Emotional Intelligence

Table of Contents

Introduction

Communication is easily the most important part of human lives. I'm sure many of us have realized this at some point of time, and if you haven't yet, it's time you did. Take a moment to really think about this and put your life into perspective. Think about each day and how you spend it, and you will soon realize that communication carries a lot of weight in your daily life. Whether or not we are aware of it, we are constantly communicating with others around us. Sometimes it is deliberate, while other times it's just instinctive. Sometimes it is verbal, while sometimes it's nonverbal. Whatever forms our communication takes, it is still communication. What does this have to do with emotional intelligence? Read on and you will see.

To be successful in our lives, we need to effectively communicate, and in that endeavor, we need to be able to control our emotions well and craft our interpersonal skills. This doesn't always come naturally. In fact, many people find this difficult because they struggle with tactlessness, introversion, or let their emotions get in the way of their communication. But most of these reasons can be fixed, or at least controlled, if you take your own emotional intelligence into account and use your knowledge of it to enhance your communication skills. In this book, *Emotional Intelligence: How to Increase EQ, Interpersonal Skills, Communication Skills and Achieve Success,* I will teach you how to hone your interpersonal skills and become more emotionally intelligent so that you can take charge of your life and be successful in achieving all your goals. You will learn how to handle a number of scenarios after reading this book. You will also find you have more control over your life. You will find yourself less limited in your responses to others and how others perceive you because your emotions are not getting in the way of your reactions to any given stimuli.

Therefore, taking control of your life is vital to your own personal level of success. People around you will respond better to you and you will find that a different approach to life makes your goals not only possible, but also probable. There is a science called neuro linguistic programing that deals with how you read and empathize with other people, which is truly useful for interpersonal communication in the workplace. However, if you want to change the way you live your life, you need to look at your emotional responses. Your emotional responses are most likely where you are going wrong.

This book covers that and shows you how to change your responses so you are fully in control of your emotions. Once you are fully in control you can use your emotions in an intelligent way to enhance your life and make your dreams come true. Think this is beyond you? It isn't. In fact, when you understand how emotional intelligence works, you can hone those skills and make life work the way you want it to, rather than having to put up with what happens during the course of your life. Don't put up with second best. Once you open your mind and take control of your emotions, you take control of your own path leading to your destiny. It really is simple. This book is devoted to showing you what emotional intelligence is all about and how you can use it to make your life a much better place to be. So let's get started.

Chapter 1:
Emotional Intelligence — The Basics

You must have heard of emotional intelligence on the Internet or from somewhere else. It's quite the buzz right now, and numerous studies are being done in this field at this very moment. But despite the words being thrown about as a potentially life changing element, not many people fully understand it. They think they do, but if you have come this far in your search for emotional intelligence, then it's obvious that you want more information.

In this first chapter, we will look at what emotional intelligence exactly *is* and why it matters. Only by first understanding this can you use it to make your life a better place to be.

What is it?

Emotional intelligence is simply the way in which someone evaluates, controls, and perceives their emotions. All human beings feel and exhibit a wide variety of emotions such as sadness, anger, happiness, and boredom, among other negative and positive human traits. We can go from one to the other in a matter of seconds, and this happens quite often in day-to-day life, as circumstances have a habit of changing. What if you could control how your emotions surfaced? Can you imagine how neat it would be if you were able to react to everything that happened to you in the same cool, calm, and collected way? Emotions can eat into our positivity, take away our incentive, and actually drive us nuts if we let them. However, once you take control of your emotions, you are able to process your life in a much more mature way, stay focused, and stay in control.

It's important, however, that all of your emotions stay in check in the long run, and that you keep them balanced. You can't always stay angry with someone you recently had a quarrel with, or remain sad over something that happened last weekend. Similarly, you can't always feel happiness, because there needs to be a place for sadness in your life, too. Sadness can teach you a lot, and you don't need to perceive it in a negative light as long as you let it pass. The problem is that people hold onto these negative thoughts until they build up. When negative emotions build up, people become negatively charged, which affects the ways we see life and new opportunities.

So you need to be in control of your emotions and know which emotions to show in what circumstances. If you're good at it, it means you possess high emotional intelligence, whereas if you struggle with it, you have low emotional intelligence and have not yet learned to take control. Some people are naturally really good at it, while others struggle without even realizing it. But that's okay. It can be worked and improved upon; you just need to be aware of how to go about it.

If you find that often you are brought down to size by your emotions, you are letting them rule your life, rather than being in control. This may happen in the case of someone who has low self-esteem or someone who is accustomed to disappointment, but until you take control and responsibility for your emotions, you can never actually be in control of them. You need to know why you feel things, so put it into perspective and accept the different aspects of emotional response, so that you are working within guidelines that are sensible. For example, if someone dies, you may respond by being sad and crying. That's an acceptable response. However, if you let that grief take hold of your everyday life to such an extent that you are unable to function — that's another thing entirely. Your emotions are not in your control and you are not able to step beyond them.

When did emotional intelligence come about?

The concept of emotional intelligence is fairly new. Yes, humans have exhibited emotions for a long, long time, but they never did much research on it until the last few decades.

It was Howard Gardener who, in 1983, realized IQ tests were simply inadequate when it came to assessing a person's true intelligence. He figured there had to be more to a person's intellect than just plain logic. That is when he devised a theory: if one wants to understand a person's true intelligence, one must also count emotional responses.

Wayne Payne coined the term "emotional intelligence" in 1985, as it is commonly believed, in his book *A Study of Emotion: Developing Emotional Intelligence*. The term became quite popular and is widely used now. Most of us call it EI or EQ, and it represents the level of a person's emotional intelligence. Higher EI means that a person's chances of communicating better with others and become successful in life are much higher. This success not only encompasses their professional lives but also extends to their social and personal lives.

Thus, people who are in control of their emotional intelligence are able to handle situations that people who lack control of their emotions are not able to handle. Therefore, you have two different human reactions that may arise from the same stimulus.

What is its purpose?

Emotional intelligence is a concept that has everything to do with a person's emotions. The purpose of it is to get an understanding of how capable a person is when it comes to identifying, evaluating, displaying, and controlling his or her emotions. Hard logic will only take you so far unless you have decent emotional intelligence. Without emotional intelligence, people can't make the most of their intelligence or their lives. Someone who possesses high emotional intelligence will build lasting relationships with others, show empathy, and be able to communicate with others comfortably, while those with lower emotional intelligence will not. Low emotional intelligence also means that an individual feels out of control in their lives and will blame circumstance, rather than bad management, for the outcome of their outpouring of emotional response.

Emotional intelligence has a different value to each of us, and the ways we choose to hone it depends upon what we need and desire the most. For example, those who deal professionally with child abuse on a day-to-day basis will know that they cannot use their own emotions and that these will get in the way of being able to make determinations in a professional capacity. Now, imagine someone with low emotional intelligence in the same job and it would be a nightmare for anyone having to deal with this professional because he or she would not know how to respond in anything but a personal manner.

I use this as a benchmark because it serves as a good one. If you want to be a professional in an area that affects your emotions, you have to be able to keep those emotions in check. For example, how do you think people who work in a hospice situation keep their cool? These people perform vital work and are constantly surrounded by others who are at the end of their lives. Now imagine someone with low emotional intelligence in a job such as this. It's quite possible that their reaction to the stimulus of death would be so negative it would negatively impact people who already are dealing with the impending loss of a loved one. This would serve very little purpose indeed.

Thus, you can see from this that there are people in life who are able to detach themselves from their emotions for the sake of work. But what if you were able to do that in your own life? Imagine the difference that you would be able to see when faced with bad situations. You take control. You are much more capable and instead of being the person who needs everyone else to be strong for you, you remain the strong person and are able to be there for the less intelligent of the species, making your value to them so much more than it would be if you had not honed your emotional intelligence.

Chapter 2:

Principles of Emotional Intelligence

Now that we understand the basics of emotional intelligence, it's time we take a look at the main principles of emotional intelligence. This chapter will talk about these principles in order to help you get a better understanding and to be able to put them to work in your own life. You will find that, with practice, it's easy to raise your emotional intelligence levels and become a much stronger person as a result.

Perceive

Understanding other people's emotions well is called the ability to perceive emotions. It's one of the most important things in emotional intelligence because it helps you form the appropriate response to counter or complement someone else's emotions. It works kind of like a trigger. Most of us perceive emotions almost automatically, but for some, it can be difficult and requires effort at times. There are various ways to perceive emotions: sight, touch, sound, expressions, body language, words, tone, and, indeed, there are many other ways. Take a look at your life and the people around you. Try to determine whether the people you observe are sad or happy just from your own observation of them. You may be asking yourself, why is this important? Signs and signals are there for everyone to grasp but not everybody does. If you have approached someone at a moment when they are not at their best for receiving your approach, you will have no doubt suffered regret and may have wished you approached at a different time. Once you exercise your emotional intelligence, you'll be able to determine a better time.

When you learn to perceive what others are feeling, this really opens up new avenues and helps you to understand situations much better than an onlooker who may be blinkered by their own thoughts, and as a result, not that empathetic toward others.

Reason

After perceiving a person's emotions, the next step is to reason with them and generate your own emotions. Someone with low emotional intelligence might counter anger by generating anger, but that's not what a person with high level of emotional intelligence would do. Instead, he or she would counter the other person's anger by remaining as calm as possible due the reasoning that takes place instantly in his or her brain.

This makes emotional intelligence a very good attribute for someone who is working in fields populated with at-risk populations. A teacher with emotional intelligence would be able to reason with children who were acting in an inappropriate manner, rather than getting mad at them. A counsellor would be able to show empathy instead of feeling fed up of listening to someone who is perpetually letting his or her emotional responses get in the way of logical responses.

Understand

Simply perceiving a person's emotions is not enough. You have to also understand why they are exhibiting those emotions. There can be a number of reasons for this and to appropriately judge the reason, you have to understand the person. This doesn't come easily, however. Most people have to devote some time and gain experience before they can become good at understanding and analyzing these traits. A mother with a good maternal instinct, who also has a high level of emotional intelligence, would be much more likely to find solutions that suit everyone, rather than resorting to shouting at a child because of her own inadequacy. Emotional intelligence, response, and understanding all help people feel more empathy. You may think empathy means being sorry for someone, but that's a misconception. Empathy means being able to put yourself in another person's shoes and being able to understand what it feels like to be in that person's situation.

Manage

In the end, it's all about managing your emotions. If you can't do that, then all the other things are useless. Therefore, managing your emotions is extremely important. There's a time to speak up and there's a time to remain calm; every situation requires a different approach. You can't react to every kind of situation without first thinking about it and managing your emotions. When you deal with a situation, your emotions must stay in sync with your thoughts and the actions that you undertake. If that doesn't happen, there's bound to be some sort of miscommunication, which will result in others getting hurt or something going wrong. It's so much easier to react without thinking, but every time you need to react, you must think about the action you are going to take. If you know there's no need to react in a certain manner, you must exercise control over your emotions.

Chapter 3:

Why Is Emotional Intelligence Important?

Psychological research lately has been rife with the concept of emotional intelligence, and this topic is being looked into extensively. People are especially interested in knowing how it affects people in the work environment. People are the ones who make up businesses, so it's natural that anything that affects people will also affect the functioning of a business. It has become so important that many people have even come to regard emotional intelligence quotient (EQ) as a better predictor of success than IQ. Many believe that it's also much more efficient at predicting quality of relationships and a person's overall happiness.

If you work it out, having employees who react in an emotional way is detrimental to a company because you can lose so many productive hours of work due to the mismanagement of emotions. When there is conflict between two employees, this is disruptive in the workplace and means that productivity will go down. Therefore, those who can keep their emotions in check are much more likely to succeed in their work without letting emotions get in the way of productivity.

The concept of emotional intelligence has come so far, and it's interesting to see its evolution throughout the years. In the 1930s emotional intelligence was referred to as "social intelligence." Then in the mid-20th century it came to be known as "emotional strength," and in the late-20th century, it got its current name, "emotional intelligence." Even though the idea has gone through name changes, it all amounts to the very same thing.

Whatever you call it, emotional intelligence is very important for us. It helps us become more self-aware, manage our emotions better, become more motivated to work towards our goals, understand others' emotions and be more empathetic, and build better relationships. It also means that the path of your life is much more straightforward and that you are less likely to err into emotional territory and ruin your own chances of success.

Importance of Emotional Intelligence

Physical Well-Being: We all know how unhealthy stress can be for our bodies. It impacts our overall wellness and has deep connections with our emotional intelligence. You must be aware of your emotional state and be able to control your emotions so you can manage stress and take care of your body. You will also find that emotional intelligence enables you to keep your blood pressure at a reasonable level without medication. When you clam up emotionally and are overtaken by stress, it is also quite likely that your oxygen levels will be unhealthy. This is because of changes to the rhythm of your breathing that happen as a result of letting emotions overtake your thinking.

Mental Well-Being: A lot of our emotional problems can be dealt with more effectively by becoming more aware of our emotional intelligence. It impacts our outlook on life and our attitude, helping to pacify anxiety and mood swings. Someone with a high level of emotional intelligence is much less likely to undergo depression, and will generally have a positive attitude in life.

You may have observed people who are able to excel even when under pressure. The reason that they are able to do this is because they are able to put their emotions into check and know that any other way of dealing with them may be detrimental. These are people who are calm and who are able to stay calm regardless of how much life provokes them to be otherwise.

Relationships: Managing our emotions and having total control over them ensures we communicate what we intend in a well thought out manner. With better emotional intelligence we understand others and relate to their feelings better. This increases the functionality of all our relationships because we understand people's needs, emotions, and responses.

People with emotional intelligence are also very much in control of their own emotions and will not let them get in the way of their life's progress. They make wonderful listeners and can often mirror logic back to people with less emotional intelligence in order to help others make sense of situations beyond their control.

Conflict Resolution: It becomes much easier to resolve any conflicts or even avoid them beforehand when we start to correctly discern people's emotions and empathize with their perspective. When we have the ability to understand the needs of others, we also get better at negotiating with them. Think about it: if you can perceive what people want, won't you find it easier to give them what they want in return for what you want?

Thus, a boss with emotional intelligence will not just take into account what *he* wants. He will know his workforce

sufficiently to know they will be looking to see "what's in it for them?" and be able to put forward new ideas and get a great response from his employees. If you look at entrepreneurs such as Richard Branson, one of the things many employees share is that Richard Branson is a man who knows what he wants and knows how to get employees what they want because he has a perpetual enthusiasm and expects people around him to be equally enthusiastic. Because he surrounds himself with people who want to succeed he gets a wonderful response from his workers. They latch onto his enthusiasm and find that they are spurred on to succeed by a man who trusts his employees to come up with solutions. Someone with emotional intelligence won't seek to be in charge and dictate to others. He or she will seek to trust people and to give them responsibilities and because of their positivity will get great results from this trust.

Success: Procrastination, low self-esteem, and lack of goal clarity are some of the biggest problems that stop us from being successful in life. When you have a high level of emotional intelligence, you also tend to have high self-confidence, drive, strong internal motivation, and clarity of your focus and goal. This, in turn, helps you overcome setbacks quicker, be resilient in different circumstances, create better support networks, and persevere. A person with high emotional intelligence sees the long-term goals and delays instant gratification, allowing them to succeed.

If you were to say you wanted to be successful, would you be able to put your perceived success into words? The problem with those who do not use emotional intelligence is that they let their emotions get in the way of seeing the bigger picture. "I want to be rich" is too vague of a statement and gives the person no real values. People who think like this usually hold themselves back because they are not able to see beyond the fact that others are rich and they are not. Thus, they will never succeed. Those who use positivity and aim it directly at goals that are tangible are much more likely to succeed.

Leadership: This is a direct benefit of understanding and empathizing with others' emotions. When you understand the emotions of people you lead, you notice things that motivate them. You create strong bonds with others at your workplace and relate to them in a positive manner, which inevitably makes you become a better leader. Recognizing the needs of others, meeting those needs to encourage high performance, and providing workplace satisfaction are some really important qualities in a good leader. When you possess high emotional intelligence, you are emotionally savvy and this helps you build stronger teams at the workplace by strategically using the emotional diversity in a team. This benefits the whole team.

Even though we still don't fully understand emotional intelligence, we can be absolutely certain that emotions play a really important role in the quality of our professional and personal lives as a whole. It can be even more critical than our general intelligence. Our ability to understand, manage, and master our emotions and those of people around us is far more important than any information technology can help us to learn. It is almost instinctive and when you learn to use it, you empower yourself no end.

Chapter 4:

Signs of High Emotional Intelligence

Have you ever wondered what is it that makes some people more successful? Intelligence Quotient and work ethics are really important, but there is one other thing that is equally important: emotional intelligence. Emotional intelligence is all about managing emotions, your own as well as of those who are around you, and this can play an important role in determining your success as well as your happiness.

Plato said that all the processes of learning have some emotional basis. He was right. The manner in which we interact with others and tend to regulate our emotions has implications in all aspects of our life. For a better understanding, emotional intelligence can be thought of as "street smarts" when compared to "book smarts" when evaluating the ability of a person to effectively navigate life. Emotional intelligence manifests itself as a person's ability of staying confident, working sincerely towards their goals, being adaptable, and flexible. A person who is emotionally intelligent can handle stress better and will always be resilient. Emotional intelligence is made up of five components: self-regulation, self-awareness, motivation, social skills, and empathy. Some might be strong in some aspects and weak in the others, but the ways of improving these can be easily learned. You will learn more about this in the coming chapters. Not really sure how to rate your emotional intelligence? Mentioned below are 14 signs that will help you decide for yourself.

Curiosity to know about others:

Do you enjoy meeting new people? Do you tend to ask questions about new people after you have been introduced? If your answer is yes, then you are empathetic to a certain degree. This is one important component of emotional intelligence. Highly Empathetic People, also referred to as HEPs, are those who are fine-tuned to pick up and then act on the needs and feelings of others. They have one thing in common: their genuine curiosity to know more about others. You can cultivate empathy by being curious about others. Curiosity tends to expand when you start talking to people outside your own social circle because you will find you get acquainted with people who have different perspectives toward things than you.

You are a good leader:

All good leaders tend to have one thing in common: their high degree of emotional intelligence combined with talent, work ethics, ambition, drive, and other such traditional characteristics of effective leaders. More than cognitive ability, emotional intelligence differentiates those who are in senior leadership roles from those who are slightly above average. The higher ranking a person is in an organization, the higher their emotional intelligence.

You know your strengths as well as your weaknesses:

A really important aspect of being self-aware is being honest with yourself about who you are, your strengths, and the areas in which you struggle. A person who is emotionally intelligent is capable of identifying their areas of strengths and weaknesses and can also analyze them to work well within the given framework. This awareness would help in building self-confidence, which is an essential ingredient of emotional intelligence. If you know what you are good at then you can play your strengths to the best advantage possible.

You can pay attention:

Do you tend to get distracted every time your phone beeps or find yourself consumed with random thoughts? If the answer is yes, then this is probably the reason that you aren't able to function at the highest level of emotional intelligence. Being able to stay focused and not let other things unnecessarily distract you is a secret for becoming emotionally intelligent. It would get really difficult to build relationships with others, and even with yourself, if you can't stay present and aware of yourself. Your ability to concentrate on the work you have to do without thinking about playing your video games, going out, or checking your phone would have a much more significant impact on your financial success in your adulthood than a higher IQ would.

You are the reason why you are upset:

Experiencing emotional fluctuations is normal and this might happen often. But more often than not you might misunderstand the reason for the anger or sadness that you are experiencing. A really important aspect of self- awareness is the ability of recognizing the underlying cause, or reason, for an emotional fluctuation, as well as the origin of those emotions. Self-awareness is also about recognizing those emotions as and when they arise, rather

than trying to ignore them. A person who is emotionally intelligent would want to take a step back and analyze where these emotions are coming from and the reason for them.

You can get along with people:

Having relationships that are fulfilling and effective are signs of emotionally intelligent people. If you think you can get along well with others and that you don't have any problem interacting with others, then your emotional quotient would be higher than the rest.

You care about being a good person:

There is one aspect of emotional intelligence that is associated with our moral personality, which is the extent we want to be able to see ourselves as ethical and caring. Regardless of how you might have acted in past situations, if you want to build on your moral individuality, then it is most likely that your EQ is high.

You slow down to help others:

If you manage to take time out and slow down a bit so you can pay attention to what others are doing, such as saying hello to someone or even helping an old lady cross the road, you are exhibiting emotional intelligence. Most of us, for most of the time, tend to focus on ourselves. This happens because we are all usually in a state of constant stress and pressure to get things done. Because of this, we simply don't notice others much, let alone help them. The spectrum goes from being completely self-absorbed to being empathetic and showing compassion. If we are always preoccupied and focus only on ourselves, then we really won't have any time for noticing others. You can start being more compassionate if you just make sure you are taking some time out of your day to see how others around you are doing instead of being self-absorbed all the time.

You can read facial expressions:

Being able to understand how others are feeling is an important aspect of emotional intelligence. Expressions tend to convey way more than words normally would. Being able to read a person's expressions would provide an insight into what is it he or she is actually thinking or feeling at a given point of time.

You can deal with setbacks:

The manner in which you deal with your setbacks and your mistakes says a lot about the you as an individual. A person who is emotionally intelligent would understand that setbacks are just a part of life, and no matter what, it is always important to keep going. Instead of viewing a setback as a failure it would be better if you can do something to get yourself back on track. You need to pick yourself up and keep going. This is part of life and you will have to be mindful of how far you let your setbacks affect you. Keep your negative emotions in check and make sure they don't go out of control; doing this will make you more resilient. A person who is resilient does not let negative emotions overtake his or her life, instead such a person lets all emotions coexist. It is about finding a bright spot even when things get dull.

You are a good judge of character:

You have always been able to judge who is good for you and who isn't and your intuitions have very rarely been wrong. Call this intuition, vibes, aura or your gut, but when you feel something is amiss, maybe there is. Trust your intuition and don't let it fade away. A person who is emotionally intelligent is capable of following his or her intuition and feels comfortable doing so. If you aren't able to trust yourself with your own emotions, what can you trust with yourself? Listen to that tiny voice within you; it won't lead you down the wrong path.

You are self-motivated:

It is not just about being ambitious, but being self-motivated. Even when you were a child, do you recall your ambitious and hardworking nature, even when there wasn't a reward to be won? If you are self-motivated, then there is very little that can stop you from achieving and doing what you want to do. Nothing works better than the motivation that comes from within.

You clearly know when to say no:

Self-regulation is about being able to discipline yourself and regulate your emotions. One of the main characteristics

of self-regulation is that you know when you need to put your foot down. People who are emotionally intelligent are capable of tolerating stress and can control their emotions.

If you exhibit most of these traits, then you are an emotionally intelligent individual. But if you feel that there is some room for improvement, start cultivating a few of the habits that have been mentioned above. Initially, you will have to make a conscious effort of following those habits, but with the passage of time they will all come naturally to you.

Chapter 5:

Main Components of Emotional Intelligence

E motional intelligence is made up of five essential components: self-awareness, self-regulation, internal awareness, empathy, and social skills.

Self-Awareness

Self-awareness can be considered to be the foundation for both personal growth as well as success. Self-awareness can be the keystone of emotional intelligence and it is one of the most powerful tools for revolutionizing one's life. If you are able to recognize and understand your emotions, then you will have the power to control them. It becomes extremely difficult for your emotions to control you when you possess this kind of self-awareness, unless you consciously decide to let them have the upper hand.

Roosevelt once said men and women aren't prisoners of their fate, but they are simply the prisoners of their own mind. This thought is the key for breaking free of the prison you have created for yourself. By being self-aware, you can choose to escape reacting to certain events and emotions, as well as train your responses for any given situation. If you have seen the TV series "Prison Break," you probably realize Michael Scofield was able to break free of the prison because he learned the system really well. In a similar manner, you needn't be a prisoner of your reactions. Your freedom also comes from understanding the system well. In this particular case, you are the system and you need to know yourself. Self-awareness, like the name suggests, is to be aware of one's own self, recognizing your emotions, strengths, and your limitations.

Before you can start making changes in yourself, you will need to know what you will be working on and the changes you should be making. Becoming self-aware is all about trying to understand yourself. Emotional awareness means you are able to recognize the emotions that you are experiencing, and as a result of this recognition, you are able to understand your thought process and the outcomes of that process. During a game, most of the professional athletes are given intensive training to assist them in recognizing and overcoming their emotions for the duration of the game. It is quintessential they don't let emotions, like frustration and anger, hamper their performance during games.

When you are aware of your strengths as well as your limitations then you will grow more confident about your capabilities. Self-confident people tend to be really assertive about what they believe is the right thing to do. Don't confuse being assertive with meaning that you get your way all the time. Being assertive means you are able to communicate your ideas and thoughts confidently while explaining to others why you believe in a particular decision.

There are three competencies that are associated with self-awareness. The first one is emotional self-awareness, which means you are capable of recognizing your emotions and the ways in which they affect your life. The second one is self-assessment, and for this you need to be able to identify your strengths and limitations. The third one is self-confidence, which means being aware of your self-worth as well as your capabilities.

Developing self-awareness

Self-awareness can be cultivated slowly. You will need to spend some time trying to understand and recognize the areas you will need to develop. You will also have to consciously **make an effort** for developing or improving particular features of yourself. Here are some ways in which you will be able to become aware of your strengths and your areas of improvement. You could start by rating yourself and think of all those areas in which you excel. You can ask others for feedback, but do this only when you can accept their feedback positively. Completing an assessment test will help you discover your personality, important traits, values, skills and abilities.

If you really want to develop your self-awareness then it would really be helpful if you could **maintain a journal** where you write down the things that are happening around you, your feelings, emotions, and your reactions. Your reaction might have been physical, emotional, or even physiological. You can make a list of the roles and feelings you would associate with each role. Think of all the different roles that you play in your life: as a wife, husband, mother, father, sister, brother, employee, employer and so on. Think of as many roles as you can and all the different feelings that you would associate with these roles. Then, **predict how you would feel** in each role. Do this by thinking about a situation you are in and then predict how you would feel in such a situation if you were in a different role. You should practice naming and even accepting those feelings. For example, you might feel frustrated, angry, or helpless. When you name these feelings you will get some control over these emotions. Once you are in control of your emotions you will be able to react in an appropriate manner.

People who are emotionally intelligent tend to plan in such a manner that they have time set aside for working on their

self-awareness. One way in which you can do this is by meditating or setting time aside for a daily reflection. In order to accomplish this, you will need to create a quiet space for yourself where you will be away from your work and other activities. Only when you are separate can you spend time focusing on your thoughts and emotions.

As you begin to become more self-aware, you can engage in a process to test how your skills are developing. You can use the ideas already outlined above such as journaling and predicting your behavior and then move on to test with the outside world if, in fact, you are accurately evaluating yourself. You can do this by engaging other people. When you have an experience such as a conversation, conflict or interaction with another, take a moment to reflect on that experience. Ask yourself what emotions arose, how you handled yourself and how you treated the other person. You can do this as a mental reflection or as a journaling exercise. Break down the experience. Consider what actually happened, what was actually said and then apply a review. Did you act appropriately? Were you calm and calculated or did you experience a sense of being swept away in your emotions and reacting automatically? Once you complete the reflection (which can take a mere few moments), check in with the person you were speaking with or someone who was in the room. Ask them open-ended questions to see if your assessment matched what was viewed by an outside person.

Ask how they thought the interaction went and how you handled yourself. You can let them know you are working on developing empathy and emotional intelligence and that you value their honest feedback. After they give you the feedback, simply thank them. By being receptive to feedback and showing your appreciation without defending yourself, you teach people around you that it is okay to give you feedback. You create a safe space for honest communication and this will mean that people will continue to help you on your path. If you defend yourself or question their reflections on the experience, they might filter what they share with you in the future. Keep in mind that they are seeing the world through their own lenses as well, and they might not be experts in emotional intelligence, but take the time to consider what they said and see how it can help you with your self-knowledge. Did you see the situation the way someone else witnessed it? You can do a follow up personal reflection, or you can journal about any discrepancies between how you saw the situation and how they did. Consider the cues that would help you better assess situations moving forward. Think about body language, what people said, if anyone raised their voice and so forth. You do not need to be perfect. You are in the process of self- development so give yourself some space to observe, learn, try new approaches and reflect.

Your assumptions, values, and beliefs shape up your individuality and your personality. **Values** can be thought of as the principles, standards, morals, ideals, and ethics that shape your life. Knowing and being aware of your values is an integral part of developing your self-awareness. When you know your values, the journey of life somehow becomes much easier and clearer. You will feel safe and secure about the direction you are heading in. You will also feel confident as well as relaxed because of the awareness that you are heading down the right path. You will also become more aware of how your values drive your emotions and your reactions. By being able to float up to 10,000 feet and look at the ways you make decisions and interact with others, you are able to see that some fundamental aspects of what you care about drive so much of your automatic behavior. You will see that when you react strongly to something that in fact, what is being said by someone else or happening in your environment is confronting your fundamental values. Or conversely, when you get the sense that other people are overreacting to something, you can see that your response may be less because the situation does not speak to your core values (or otherwise aligns with them). You may also notice other people's reactions and begin to draw connecting lines between their reactions and what could potentially be their core values. By being active in observing your own and other's reactions, you become more literate of yourself and others. You will start to see behind the curtain of the magic show. You may find yourself reacting less strongly to situations because you are more aware of what is happening in your own mind and body. You take yourself out of the role of the reactionary person and become the observer, which then can lead you to respond in a more considered and possibly articulate manner.

It is very common that everyone has got certain **assumptions** about those around them, but it is really important you are aware of the assumptions that you have about others. This is an important aspect of emotional intelligence and it does not mean that you ignore the assumptions you have about your own self. Assumptions about your own self can be positive as well as negative. Negative assumptions are those thoughts that keep pulling you down or stopping you from doing something different. Thoughts like, "I can't start my own business because I don't have sufficient knowledge," or even something like "Bad things always seem to follow me." Instead of these thoughts, replace them with positive assumptions like, "If I keep trying without giving up, I will definitely be successful." Try this simple exercise to understand whether or not you have a positive assumption about yourself. Spend some time and think of any challenging task that you have had to perform recently. It could be anything related to your personal or professional life. Think about this event and recollect the immediate thoughts that you had regarding your ability for completing the task. If the immediate thoughts that you had were positive, then how do you think this influenced the way in which you went about completing the task? If you think that your immediate thoughts had been negative, then that is alright. But take some time and think about how these thoughts made you feel when you were completing the work. Also think about the manner in which you can turn those thoughts into positive ones the next time. Whenever you come up with a solution or suggestion that can help you along the next time, take a moment and write it down. The beliefs we hold about ourselves are extremely important and they help determine our mindset and our behavior. You start to see yourself as having a choice in not only what you think, but also how you feel and react in a given situation. Adding choice means that you are in control and not taken by surprise by your emotions. You get to analyze what is happening within yourself and within others and then test your assumptions. After some time, you will become an expert at finding clues to see if your assumptions are based in reality or created by your mind. Our minds are constantly adding to what is actually happening. So when someone says something, for example, our mind draws on our past experiences and also looks for where our fears or worries play into the current circumstance. This is a very animalistic reaction, something that our brains do in order to keep us safe. That said, for the most part, when we are conscious and alert, there are very few real dangers in our interactions with others. So this is why learning to be aware of our assumptions can help us determine what is real versus what our brains add automatically. When we can separate the reality of what is happening from all of the added "stories", we become much abler to deal with real situations and less reactionary based on our animalistic machinery. At this level of functioning, even when emotions creep up, we are able to analyze why those emotions emerge and then we can choose to react consciously.

Self-Regulation

"The Two Wolves" is a Native American story that begins with an old Cherokee telling his grandson about the constant battles continuously going on within a person's mind. He says the battle is between two wolves. One of the wolves is the evil one; it is jealous, envious, angry, distressed, greedy, arrogant, ignorant, inferior, deceitful, self- pitying, guilty, proud, remorseful, narcissistic, and superior. The other wolf is the good one; it is happy, serene, enduring, empathetic, loving, kind, benevolent, humble, generous, honest, diplomatic, and faithful. The grandson thinks for a while and then quietly asks his grandfather which wolf has won the battle? The old Cherokee smiles and says the wolf you feed will win.

The moral of the story is simple: you will always have two choices in any given situation and the way you react depends upon you. You can react in either a positive or a negative manner. If you start practicing thinking positively and behaving in a positive manner, then negativity wouldn't really be able to affect your thinking or your behavior. You can apply the story of the two wolves to your workplace. Think of a situation where you have been passed over for a promotion. You could start thinking negatively about your boss and all that negativity would start affecting your work. Or you can calm yourself down, take a few deep breaths, fill your mind with positive thoughts, and keep telling yourself something better will come along your way, that the person deserving the job got it this time and the decision your boss made wasn't personal. Positive thoughts will help you think more clearly and help you get a clear perspective of reality. You will need to think and make a conscious decision regarding which of the wolves you want to feed and your behavior will change accordingly. If you decide to feed the good wolf, then you will be able to manage how you feel, act and behave, all of which will help in regulating yourself.

Self-regulation is all about being able to keep all your disruptive emotions, thoughts, and impulses in check in order to think things through before acting. This is one of the five essential ingredients that make up emotional intelligence. People who are capable of self-regulation see the good that exists in others and can identify opportunities in any given situation. They always tend to keep the lines of communication open, make their motives known, their intentions clear from the beginning, and will act according to the values in which they believe. They will also always work to the very best of their abilities and are capable of ensuring things come to a logical conclusion even when the going gets tough. Persons who can self-regulate themselves will always be able to cheer themselves up when they are feeling blue and even calm themselves down when they are angry or upset. They are really flexible and can adapt to any environment they are put in, regardless of the people with whom they have to work. They also like taking charge of a situation whenever it is necessary. One of the most important skills that a leader requires is emotional intelligence, because it provides the awareness not only of one's own emotions but also of the emotions of others. Self-regulation is also important because it helps you manage ways you react and express your thoughts, opinions, and yourself in an appropriate manner at any given point of time.

You will be able to perform when you are able to manage and control your emotions and impulses. It is important to act in harmony with your social conscience, rather than doing what you might want to do. For instance, you might have a lot of official workload, but when you see your teammate struggling with their work you might help them out. Self-regulation would also stop you from behaving in a manner that would cost you, your team, and the organization you work for, even thought there might be short-term benefits that are associated with the behavior. Self-regulation is about delaying gratification you would receive by doing something impulsive just because there is a short-term benefit associated with it. If you are able to think clearly and suppress your emotions for the time being, then you would be able to think ahead and figure out the possible consequences of doing what you were about to do. For instance, you can turn down an invitation to a party because you are working on an important assignment. Or perhaps you are reigning in your emotions when all that you really want to do is tell a difficult team member your true opinion of them. Self-regulation also means you are able to overcome any negative feedback you might have received without wasting time wallowing in self-pity and letting that self-pity affect your work. If others are able to see you are in complete control of your emotions and that you can keep calm even in stressful circumstances, then the chances of them handing out important work and projects to you increases. You will be perceived as an individual who both is approachable and dependable.

Developing self-regulation:

You can always work on developing your self-regulation skills. In this section we will take a look at the eight strategies that will help you in developing it.

Managers tend to be better role models when they practice what they preach. They can create an environment conducive to enhancing productivity if they are self-regulated, and if they **lead with honesty.** This means always doing the right thing for the right reasons, even when it isn't the easiest available option. People who have integrity and display the same in their life as well as work tend to be more successful because the ones around them respect them. If you want to behave with integrity, then you will have to recognize the values that are dear to you. Your values are those things you would never want to give up on, however testing the times get, and even when sticking to your values proves to be a disadvantage. You will need to realize you will sometimes lose out on opportunities because you chose to be ethical, but your efforts will pay off in the long run. You will need to start living your life according to your core values and you will need to start admitting your mistakes, take responsibility for the things you do, and listen to your conscience. People tend to treat others the way they treat them. If you don't want to be at the receiving end of any unpleasantness, then you need to start being good to others. If you can stay positive and optimistic even during trying circumstances, then those around you will also be able to stay calm when things get rough.

People who can self-regulate themselves are be able to **cope with any change** and adapt to any circumstance and behave in accordance with what is required in any given situation. Instead of seeing any change as an inconvenience, they think of change as an opportunity for development and a chance for proving themselves. People who tend to defy change can experience a lot of unpleasantness, stress, and many other negative and psychological manifestations that are unpleasant. If you want to cope with any change then you can make a SWOT analysis to see what good can come out of it. This will help you analyze the situation to decide how you can cope with it and understand the effect it would have on you, as well as the new opportunities that it would present and the ways in which you can get rid of any threats.

One of the most important aspects of self-regulation is that you need to **be aware of your weaknesses** and the ways in which the behavior of those around you affects your own behavior in a potentially negative way. You will need to be able to identify all of your triggers and make a list of all of the times when you have given in to your impulses. When you have been able to identify the emotions and the corresponding reactions that didn't prove to be useful, then you can start replacing these with reactions and emotions that are desirable. For instance, you might realize that you tend to be cranky and snap at those around you when the pressure you are under increases or when you feel stressed. In such a situation you can take some time out so you can think things through before unnecessarily snapping at others. You can maintain a stress diary where you can write down the situations that stress you out and the manner in which you think you can tackle that problem.

Look at your peaks and your valleys. Take a look at your life and think about your peak experiences as well as your low points with regard to self-regulation. Your peak experiences are those where you feel a sense of control and where you were able to assess and take action in a considered manner. Your valleys are those experiences where you perhaps walked away after you reacted to something asking yourself "what happened?" Those are experiences when you were emotionally reactionary and did not consciously choose to act. Instead, you acted from your brain's machinery without being an active player in deciding how you were going to move forward. When you reflect on both your peaks and your low points, take stock of your personal state of mind and body as well as the circumstances. Write down anything about your physical experience at the time. So return to whether you were hungry, tired or other physical experiences. Think about your state of mind at the time. Were you feeling confused, judged or stressed? Then scrutinize the circumstance and environment. Who were you with? Were you in a safe place? If you place yourself back in that situation, what were all of your senses experiencing? Going through this analysis can be helpful in pinpointing what leads you to perform well or poorly. You start to see themes such as what people, circumstances or emotions lead you to act in certain ways. This doesn't mean you have to strategically set up your world so you will always have the perfect mindset or ideal external conditions. However, it does allow you to plan better for your triggers. If you want to develop better self-regulation and avoid your low points or valley experiences, you can set yourself up to be in a good mental state before entering a circumstance that had traditionally triggered you to act poorly. You might make sure you are well-rested, well-fed or have meditated before entering a meeting for example. You begin to build awareness and resiliency to some of your triggers simply by bringing them into conscious awareness.

Self-regulation is really important if you want to achieve your long-term goals. People who are capable of showing initiative and who are able to work towards finding a solution for any challenging situation will eventually succeed. You can develop self-regulation by **working on your self-discipline.** Persistence and self-discipline go hand in hand. They will help you keep working hard and staying focused even when the going gets tough and even when you don't feel like working, or when your goals seem too distant and impossible to achieve. Instead of worrying about the long haul, think of what it would feel like when you achieve your goal and when you'll be able to enjoy the benefits of all your hard work. Self-discipline can be conceived of as working out a muscle. Each time you set a goal and take an action that leads to the likely outcome that the goal will be achieved, you become a better master of your own life and life experiences. You reinforce your ability to craft your outcomes and environment as opposed to reacting to what is happening around you. When you act in accordance to what you want in life, your brain becomes stronger at making the connection between action and result. This helps with self-regulation because you continually build on your ability to bring to your immediate awareness what your bigger goals are and you can use this as a springboard for determining your current actions. Put more simply, while you are aware that your actions lead you closer or further from your goals, you can determine how to act in any given circumstance to align best with what you want in your life. For example, if you are aware that you want to help a family member with a problem then you can be an active listener as they share and use cues in their verbal and body language that can cue you to being able to assist them appropriately. If you don't engage with awareness, you might react to them, get angry, or say things that will not send you down a path of helping them and in fact could do the opposite (i.e. push them away, hinder their sharing, etc.).

If you want to become self-regulated, then you will need to make a conscious effort regarding the wolf you would want to feed. If you feel any negativity creeping up on you, then you will need to tune the negativity out of your mind and **reframe all your negative thoughts.** Think hard and decide if the negative thoughts you are having are actually reasonable or if you are just unnecessarily being pessimistic.

Consider a situation where you were passed over for a promotion. What if the reason wasn't because you weren't good enough or because your colleague was more deserving than you, as you might have originally believed? You can make use of affirmations, as well as visualization techniques, for managing all the negative thoughts you might have about yourself. By doing this you will be able to control the manner in which you would probably react to similar situations henceforth. When you can start analyzing a situation rationally, then you will be able to undo all the damage negative thinking has caused. You can start out by simply saying you can cope with a situation and you can do better instead of just writing yourself off as a lost cause. Another strategy you can adopt is to do something positive, to shift your perspective about yourself a little, and then you will be able to look at any given situation in a positive manner and stay optimistic. For instance, if you have received some negative feedback, instead of letting all the negativity engulf you, think of the ways in which you will be able to transform the negative feedback into positive feedback. If you think there is some truth to the negative feedback, then come up with ways in which you can improve your performance next time around. If there really wasn't anything wrong on your part, then it would be helpful to approach the person who gave you the negative feedback and sort out any misunderstandings that might exist. A lot of times our negative thinking is more a product of our own mental machinery and may or may not be incited by an interaction with someone else. So reframing our thinking from negative to positive isn't a process of sweeping your emotions under the rug. Optimism can be helpful when based in reality. So start by looking at where there is a nugget of truth in your negative thinking. So if your thought is that you are terrible at your job, then start by looking in reality about where you might need more skill development for example. This is not about ruminating in the negative, but rather an exercise in moving your thinking into a more realistic perspective. Then consider how the opposite of that thought may be true and look for evidence. So in this case, map all of the things that you are good at in your job. Think about the ways you are efficient, effective, creative, useful and so forth. Then find a new thought, through this process of reframing that feels more positive, more accurate and more empowering. Again, don't deny that there may be some room for improvement or some nugget of truth in that initial negative thought. But here we want to shed the dark cloud over our thinking and choose a new thought that resonates. So it could be "I have great people skills and carry out my work with integrity and efficiency and I also produced a poor report last week that resulted in my boss giving me negative feedback." So the use of "AND" is an excellent tool in reframing a negative thought into a positive one. When we use "BUT", then we tell ourselves that if one thing exists then everything else follows in the same vein. So if we say "I am a good employee, but I am bad at research reports," then everything that follows the "BUT" becomes the more important part of the sentence. When we say "I am a good employee and I am bad at research reports," the tone of the sentence changes. Suddenly we can see that both can exist at the same time. So if you are having trouble reframing, start by writing out your "BUT" sentences. Once you have completed that, cross out the "BUT" and add in "AND". Then re-read the phrases. Your cognitive experience will be entirely different. You will find yourself coming up with solutions rather than ruminating in the negative thinking and that sense of being stuck. Taking on this process of reframing is perfectly aligned with developing your ability to self-regulate because it puts you back in the driver's seat of your emotional experience. Your emotions link to your thinking and thus guide how you interact with the world. When you are being negative, you will interact with the world in a way that treats those negative thoughts as facts. So if you think little of yourself, you act in a way that confirms that idea and therefore you often manifest interactions with others that confirm your negative thinking. When you engage in a process of reframing, you put the brakes on going down that type of negative rabbit hole. You instead change the trajectory of your emotions, thinking and behavior that will result in more positive experiences that align better with your overall goals.

Self-regulation is all about **keeping calm even under pressure**. If you think you are in a situation where you aren't able to control your emotions, try to physically or mentally get yourself out of the situation for a few minutes until you are able to calm yourself down. Although it seems unconventional at first, verbalizing your need to have a few minutes can be really useful to the others that you are interacting with. So state "let me just take a couple of minutes so I can process this and come back with some fresh thinking." There is nothing inappropriate about this, and it shows your commitment to respectful and thoughtful communication. The alternative could be getting angry or frustrated and saying things you will regret later. By taking this moment to think, process, check in with your emotions and come up with ideas on your own, you are becoming a master of self-regulation. You are acknowledging when you feel your emotional machinery kicking it, and you are pressing the pause button. At the same time, you are providing the others involved an opportunity to slow down their thinking and reacting a bit as well. If you feel your emotions are overflowing, you can make use of relaxation techniques like deep breathing or counting from one to ten slowly. This will help you cut through any negativity and put yourself back on the right track. Take in a few deep breaths and breathe out slowly, and with each breath that you are exhaling visualize that you are pushing all the unnecessary negativity out of your mind and your body.

If you feel like you are stuck in a really difficult situation or if you are trying really hard to not act on your impulses, think before you proceed and **consider the likely consequences** of your action. Think of those situations in the past when you had given in to your temptations and the outcome was not so pleasant. This will help you understand the importance of self-regulation. The other thing you can do is visualize how you look or behave when you are not in control of any situation. This will help clear up your perspective. If you feel like you are about to shout at your colleague, think of how you would look while doing so and if it is something that you would want others to see.

You will need to start **believing in yourself,** even when no one else does. Self-efficacy is a really important component of self-regulation. This is the belief you have about yourself; namely that you are capable of achieving what you set your mind to achieve. This will also help in improving your self-confidence. Think about all those situations where you were successful in the past and this will help you have a positive outlook about the situation and figure out a way to get out of it as well. You will have to make a conscious decision to believe in yourself and surround yourself with people who are confident and positive. The more you see how successful others are, the more you will feel like becoming like them.

You will also want to start believing in yourself and replace self-doubt with self-confidence. Self–regulation is all about controlling negative impulses and deciding the ways in which you want to act in any given situation. It is also about retaining your integrity and not compromising on your values and goals while you are trying to stay self-disciplined.

Internal Motivation

One of the most important characteristics of internal motivation is a keen interest in learning. It is also the search for improving yourself and of obtaining wealth and status. The only reason why people do what they do is because of their motivation. It could be your work, your hobbies, interests, your relationships, or even something as simple as fulfilling your basic needs. All these are motivations for you to behave or act in a certain manner in order to achieve something. This section will help you understand the sources of motivation and the manner in which you can develop it internally.

Motivation is of two types and you can classify them in any manner that you would want. The simplest way would be to classify them as positive and negative motivation. An even more simpler classification could be pain and pleasure. Every act that we perform, every thought that we have, and every belief that we hold has a foundation in either pain or pleasure. The concept of pain and pleasure varies from one individual to another. The associations we make towards pain and pleasure are all buried deep in our subconscious, though most people never tend to realize this. Instead of going through life on autopilot, it would really be helpful if you take a look around and think about why you are doing something instead of just doing it. It really isn't difficult to learn and shift the way you perceive a given situation. What might seem like a problem can be turned into an opportunity with just a little bit of practice. Therefore, it is safe to say that **all motivation is internal motivation**. If you believe there is more pleasure than pain to gain from an experience, then your motivation for that particular act will increase. If you believe something will just bring you pain, then the chances of you going ahead and doing that thing are much lower.

If you want to be able to change your motivation and maneuver it in your favor, then you will have to work on **reframing your associations**. For instance, if you want to shed a few pounds but you just aren't motivated to exercise, then here are some assumptions you might have that are holding you back from doing what you ought to do. You might be of the opinion that exercise has never really worked out for you; that working out a gym makes you feel bad when you compare yourself with others; that you don't have enough time for exercising and even if you did, it really wouldn't make any difference; or that you have more fun when you are relaxing and indulging in an activity that you enjoy more than exercising. There are steps for reframing the associations that exist in your mind. The first step would be to replace the pain with pleasure. Most of the assumptions in the above example were associated with pain, with the last one alone associated with pleasure, but the pleasure was not related to the task on hand. It is an obvious deduction that there are more associations with pain than with pleasure and this would mean that the person associates exercising with pain. There is an immediate need for reframing those assumptions to try to see pleasure in exercising instead of pain. Here are some instances that might help: think along the lines that if exercising can work for others, then it can work for you as well; if you go to a gym you can see others who have managed in creating an exercising routine; instead of thinking of others' successes as a competition think of it as being inspiring. Every time you exercise, you are taking a step towards a healthier life and it will eventually make you feel good. You could always consider taking up some fun exercises and involving yourself in other activities that interest you and that will provide the necessary exercise that your body needs.

The second step is that you will need to add in some pain to all the pleasure that you have been thinking about. Now that you have managed to turn all the pain points associated with exercising into pleasure points, this would prove to be sufficient motivation for some to get started. But others might need a little more motivation. Think of all the pain you would experience if you *don't* exercise. Here are certain examples that will help you get a better understanding: you would get fat without exercise and you won't be able to achieve the body you have always wanted; you won't be able to lead a healthier life since exercising isn't a habit of yours; you won't be a good role model for your family members who look up to you. You can keep going until you have managed to inspire and motivate yourself to work harder. The associations you have can be a really strong influence in determining whether or not you have the motivation for achieving the things that you want.

You will need to **get out of your comfort zone** if you want to do something new. You will need to motivate yourself to step out of the shell you have created for yourself if you want to embrace change and try something different. People tend to get really comfortable with the way things are and they stop trying to look for new ways in which they can challenge themselves for their own development. We tend to become complacent with the way things are, with our lives, and all the things that seem to have an effect on us. You need to realize you have the power and the choice of making any changes you want, and then you can start taking control of your own life. But all this requires a lot of self-motivation. You can make use of the all these techniques for taking charge of your life by staying motivated and by keeping control of positive motivation. You will have to take that one step to get out of your comfort zone if you want to do great things and have experiences that make you feel satisfied.

Empathy

Empathy can be described as the ability of understanding the emotional reaction of another person. Showing empathy is possible only when one is aware of oneself, because you can't understand others if you don't understand your own self. From the basic interactions to all the global conflicts, we seem to have hit rock bottom when it comes to compassion. You might lose a lot of things but is it really possible to let go of empathy? Well, it actually is possible. Empathy is the ability of placing yourself in the shoes of other people for understanding their feelings and their outlook of things, and this quality seems to be diminishing. The evidence of decline in empathy is startling, it isn't restricted to any city or country, and it's all across the world. Terrorism, wars, murders and all crimes against humanity and the society as a whole are instances of lack of empathy. What can you do for turning this situation around? Is it possible to learn to cultivate empathy? A recent study shows that we all have the ability to empathize and this is hardwired in our brains. In the world where it's all about hyper individualism and online culture, it really is important to work on regenerating empathy.

Stop and listen: The next time when you are arguing with your partner, parents, neighbor, colleague or anyone in general, why don't you just stop for a minute and try to listen instead? Listen to what the other person needs and their feelings. Give them a chance for expressing those particular feelings and needs, and try recollecting what they would have said so that they know that you have understood them. This will help in reducing the tension regardless of where you are. You can resolve a conflict at least 50% faster in the case of a dispute or a disagreement; both the parties in the dispute could repeat what the other had said.

Start a conversation with a stranger: One barrier to empathy is all the stereotypes as well as prejudices that we tend to have about others and these are simply based on irrelevant things like their appearance or even accent. Once you reserve your judgement about a person, you might realize that you were actually wrong about them. After all, what is it that you really know about the heavily tattooed lady who delivers your mail? Or the quiet accountant at your work who is always by himself? You can indulge yourself in conversations with complete strangers once a week and have a conversation that goes beyond simple superficial talk.

Look at things from other's perspective: You will never really understand what the other person is feeling or experiencing if you cannot put yourself in their shoes and see the situation through their eyes. This is the best way to be empathetic towards someone, only when you understand what a person is feeling will you be able to truly understand him or her.

Look into a person's eyes: The benefits of being empathetic need not be restricted to one's personal life alone, it can help in improving one's professional life as well. Empathy helps in encouraging teamwork, leadership skills, and the exploration of creative ideas. It is always helpful to have a workforce that is empathetic towards one another because they will all understand another person's viewpoint. An empathy test during the recruitment process will help in finding individuals who are emotionally intelligent, but empathy isn't easy to measure. Just as eyes are the window to the soul of a person, words and behaviors can be manipulated and controlled. If you really want to understand what another person truly feels, just look into his or her eyes.

Start teaching empathy skills: The most effective way in which you can ensure that you can reverse the substantial decline in empathy is by teaching empathy skills in the classroom. There are different activities that can be adopted for making sure that individuals are more empathetic towards each other. For instance, the Roots Program that was started in Canada has proven to be especially helpful in making children understand the emotions of others.

Empathy might be on a decline but there are different ways in which it can be brought back, not just for the development of an individual but also for the sake of the society.

Social Skills

Identifying different social cues for establishing common ground so that it helps in managing and building networks as well as relationships can be referred to as social skills. Having emotional maturity in this particular aspect manifests itself as the person's ability to listen and reason appropriately in any given situation, the ability of an individual to guide as well as inspire others, and their ability to sort out any difficult situations through their persuasive and negotiation skills.

A social skill is a very broad term that includes a lot of different concepts, but this is one aspect that has a significant effect on the emotional intelligence of a person. In the concept of emotional intelligence, social skills signify all

those skills required for handling and influencing the emotions of others. Before jumping to the conclusion that this sounds like manipulation, wait for a moment and think about it. A simple instance of this would be smiling at people. When you smile at someone it typically makes them smile back at you. This doesn't sound manipulative, doesn't it? However, this is simply positive reinforcement.

Social skills can be thought of as the final piece of the jigsaw that completes emotional intelligence. Emotional intelligence starts with your ability to understand yourself and your emotions (self-awareness), moves on to managing those thoughts and emotions (self-regulation) and making use of this for achieving the goals that you have set for yourself (self-motivation). Once you understand yourself, you can start to understand and analyze the feelings and emotions of those around you (empathy), and then finally use your ability to influence the way they think and behave (social skills). There are various skills that constitute social skills. With regard to emotional intelligence, social skills include leadership skills, communication skills, persuasion skills, conflict management skills, change management skills, ability to establish a rapport, collaboration, and cooperative skills.

Persuasion Skills

Persuasion is the ability of a person to motivate others and win them over with your ideas or the proposed course of action you want to take. People who are persuasive or who have the ability to influence are capable of picking up on the emotional undertones in any situation and are capable of putting things across in such a manner so it appeals to others.

Communication Skills

Communication skills are of extreme importance for emotional intelligence. It is not only essential that you are a good listener but you should also be able to communicate your thoughts and feelings to others as well. A good communicator is capable of not only listening to those around them but also makes sure they have understood what was being said and encourage the sharing of information openly. It is essential you are willing to listen to problems others are facing and not just the good. You must deal with all issues right away so problems don't start piling up. Along with registering all the emotional cues while communicating, you must also make sure what you are saying conveys your emotions and feelings.

Conflict Management Skills

Conflicts and disagreements can crop up at any given point of time and they can simply appear out of the blue. Managing and solving conflicts is nothing short of an art. This is really important, not just in your professional life, but in your personal life as well. You will need to understand that tact and diplomacy are two incredibly important skills when resolving conflicts. When managing a conflict, you will need to be able to bring the conflict into the open to try to resolve it. Sharing emotions is really important, as is having open discussions about the conflict. This promotes letting the undercurrents and problems come to the surface. Once everything is out in the open it gets easier to resolve a conflict because each of the parties is finally tuned in to understand what the other party feels.

Leadership Skills

It might sound strange that leadership skills have been included in the list of social skills. Shouldn't emotional intelligence be a part of leadership and not the other way around? The answer is both leadership skills and emotional intelligence are connected. As I mentioned earlier, only those individuals who are aware of their own emotions will be able to understand the emotions and influence those around them. One of the key aspects of leadership is the ability to influence others and take them along with you in the direction that you are headed in. Some people might think of this as charisma, but it is really good emotional intelligence and nothing else. Good leaders are not only able to articulate a vision but they are also able to encourage others with that vision. They don't need to be in a position of official leadership to prove they are a good leader, instead they support and guide their colleagues while holding them responsible for their actions and making sure they always lead by example.

Change Management Skill

Change managers are also known as change catalysts and these individuals help in making a certain change happen without having to alienate those who are involved in it. Change has always been stressful for all those who are involved in it. A good change catalyst presents change as an opportunity and an exciting experience for development rather than a threat. A good change catalyst is capable of recognizing where change is required and then removes all the barriers to change. A change manager always leads from the front, setting the mood for the desired change.

Building Bonds

It is really important to not just build relationships with others but also to maintain them. Developing this skill results in having better relationships, translates into better work, and with getting on with things in life. People who are good at building bonds and establishing rapport are considered to be good at networking and building and maintaining a strong web of contacts and connections. It is not just about establishing a good rapport but also about working hard to maintain established relationships. One noticeable quality of people with this skill is they have a great number of friends amongst colleagues at work. It is all about valuing others, being interested in the work they do, and having the curiosity to know more about them.

Teamwork:

There are some individuals who work really well with others and then there are those who work well when they are on their own. The ones who work well with others always want to build good relationships that prove to be productive. Cooperation and collaboration are essential ingredients of social skills. The people who can make relationships last value people as much as they value work or even more so. Active collaboration, the sharing of plans and ideas, and working together for building a better work environment are commonly their goals. While doing so, they tend to promote a cooperative atmosphere where everyone can contribute freely and can look for opportunities which helps in increasing teamwork. The team tends to perform better when there are good team workers on the team. This is because they involve all the members of the team and encourage them to collaborate. They help in establishing the identity of the team, which helps foster commitment. They might do this from any role that they hold, whether it's the role of a leader or that of a subordinate. But having people like this is essential for the success of any team.

Social skills are very important for emotional intelligence, but this doesn't start with social skills nor does it end with it. Emotional intelligence is a cycle and the core of this concept is the individual. Only those who are capable of handling and managing their emotions are capable of understanding and working along with others. Understanding this concept is crucial for developing emotional intelligence.

Chapter 6:

Emotional Intelligence in the Workplace

In the previous chapter, we read about the main principles that guide emotional intelligence. In this chapter, we will discuss how you can use emotional intelligence in your workplace to improve your own productivity. After all, this book sets out not only to describe emotional intelligence, but to teach you to harness it so that you improve your life by becoming self-fulfilled and happy.

Understand yourself

Understanding yourself is the first and foremost thing you must do to get a better idea of what you are capable of with your emotional intelligence. Once you get a fair idea of the level of your emotional intelligence, you will know how well you are able to emote. To understand how well you handle your emotions, observe yourself for a week and take a note of how well you react to certain situations. Then analyze this behavior by writing everything down that created an emotional response within you. Alternatively, you can ask someone to do the same for you. All of this will end up giving you a better understanding of your emotions.

For example, on a Monday morning, if you are given too much work to do, how do you respond? You need to recognize your negative responses and the consequences of your negativity. The kind of things that upset you in the workplace should be noted so that you can recognize them and do something about them in the future. These can include:

Personality clashes —
what was said and how
you responded Clashes
with management —
what happened and how
you responded Stresses
that invoked emotional
response
Disappointments that made you feel unhappy

You may not know it at this stage, but the way that you respond to any given stimulus affects the ways in which you carry on throughout the day. Negative feelings will bring about negative reactions. How long do you keep that negativity inside of you? Are you able to let go of it? Are you harboring bad feelings for anyone in the workplace? Record it, because even if you don't know it at the moment, you will learn that you are the cause of your own unhappiness, for your responses dictate what is happening in your life. People with lower emotional intelligence will always blame, without being able to see that it's the response itself that dictates the level of your happiness, rather than the actual trigger of the feelings that you encountered.

Adapt yourself

After completing this task of understanding your emotions comes adaptation. You need to adapt yourself to your surroundings. One generally likes a person who is like-minded, so even at your workplace you must find a group of people that have a similar mindset as you. If you are with a group where disagreements happen frequently, then it simply means their level of emotional intelligence is different from yours. Try finding a group whose emotional intelligence coincides with yours. Not only will it help you grow as a team, it will also increase your productivity. But in case you cannot find any such people or have to work with people with less emotional intelligence than you, try and change yourself in order to adapt to your environment. That means that you must be willing to adapt. People with high emotional intelligence are able to do this without compromising their basic belief system. They tolerate the actions of others while understanding that it's only because other people are working at a lower emotional intelligence and are trying to cause ripples. You need to smooth out those ripples and rise above them, rather than allowing yourself to be dragged into them.

Empathize with others

A part and parcel of emotional intelligence is empathy. It is one of those elite qualities that can either make or break your emotional intelligence. When you perceive an emotion, you must not try to rebel against it. Instead you should empathize and try and understand why a person may be feeling the way he or she does. Here's an example: someone at the office is sad because they made a mistake, resulting in a project being rejected. Empathize with that person and say something comforting instead of saying something mean and blaming the person for their mistake. Here's where one can actually distinguish a person with a high emotional intelligence from someone with less emotional intelligence. The person low-level emotional intelligence blames whereas a person with a high level of emotional intelligence empathizes and helps others grow, rather than makes them feel bad about their actions. They will get better results by empathizing and will also be able to teach their workforce to respond in a better manner, thus creating better results.

Listen to them

How does it feel when the person you're talking to is not listening? Bad. Period. We almost immediately start hating them. Now, we definitely do not want others to feel the same when we listen. In that case, make sure you start paying attention to what others are saying. What's the word for it? Listening. It is the key to good relationships and to communication, which is effective. In order to judge people's emotions and generate emotions of your own, you have to pay attention. You might generate the wrong sort of emotions if you don't, or at least that's what the people around might think. It's the only way to properly understand what emotion is guiding people. These emotions matter more than the words. Remember, if you really want to get ahead, you need to take note of these and be aware of them.

Anticipation

Anticipation, simply put, means having an idea beforehand about a particular thing or situation. In this context it means anticipating what the other person might say and the emotion behind it. It helps to be ready and prepared with a preconceived notion about what might be said so you can develop a preset mindset. But take care only to implement your thought if it matches theirs. You can always form another emotion and generate a different thought if it doesn't. By anticipating, you can communicate faster and in a better and efficient manner, while saving time. This helps when you want something from an employee or from your boss. If you have an idea about how your boss will react, you have him or her at a disadvantage and can gauge your question in such a way that it addresses his or her problems at the same time. An example of this is:

"I know your feelings about Monica, but I would like her to be involved in the team and will take full responsibility for her actions."

Thus, you have acknowledged your boss's negative feelings toward the employee and have made it clear that you are willing to help out with something that he or she sees as being potentially problematic.

Accept differences

No two people in the world are emotionally the same. There will be a lot of people who will have different mindsets, especially in the workplace. Not everyone thinks the same way. It is up to you to accept differences and embrace them. For example: after the loss of the project, there might be some who will be sad about it and show that sadness with apathy and negativity, while others won't be affected by it at all and will embrace it as a learning curve. You must be able to relate to and encourage both types, not only the type you think is right or the one you think feels the same way you do.

Use the differences

You can use differences to everyone's advantage. Work toward establishing an understanding among employees, and group them according to the kind of emotions they tend to exhibit. This will ensure better communication between teams and give them more competition that will nurture their participation and make positive things happen.

Know how to delegate

When in an office, if you want to lead with emotional intelligence, then you must be able to delegate work. Richard Branson, as mentioned in a previous chapter, is able to do this. Once he has passed a problem to an employee, he considers himself out of the loop until the solution is found. He places that much trust in his employees.

You have to understand other people's capacities and then give them the right amount of work. This will help increase productivity as a whole. You will be able to communicate with your workers better, as they will be open to listening to what you have to say. This free-flowing communication will make it easier for you to carry out your daily business duties and allow you to lead an easy and efficient work life.

Delegate power

Delegating only your work will not give you the best results. You need to delegate power because this fosters better relationships. This will give people some sense of authority, allowing them to make their own decisions in turn increasing the efficiency of their work. But prudence is a real requirement while doing this. The person to whom you are delegating the work and power should have a good sense of emotional intelligence to undertake responsibility. If you end up delegating responsibility to someone who is not capable enough, then you might be in trouble. Consider spending a considerable amount of time getting to know each of your employees in order to know his or her level of emotional intelligence.

Be just as responsible

There comes a time when you will have to take a certain part of the blame. You cannot keep running away from it and must be able to handle your emotions well. Many bosses will refrain from taking the blame even if it is their fault or if they have done something that contributes to things going wrong. This will only create problems in the workplace and to avoid this, it is best that you hone your emotional intelligence. Humility and compassion are some of the qualities that will help you achieve this. Never be afraid to say you did something wrong. It doesn't weaken you. In fact, it strengthens your position. People can relate to others who understand their own boundaries and are more likely to respect them.

Being "whiter than white" doesn't endear you to others. They need to be able to relate to you in some way. Being open and honest with them will help you to create the kind of relationship where trust is part and parcel of the situation. That's vital if you want to make the most of workplace experiences and relationships.

Chapter 7:

Emotional Intelligence for Stronger Relationships

Have you ever felt really overwhelmed by the emotions you were feeling and then said something you regretted the minute you said it? Well, this happens more frequently than many care to admit. Who hasn't had at least one moment with a lapse in judgment when they were overcome by emotions and said something that could potentially ruin something good?

The simple truth is we could all probably benefit from learning how to control and handle our emotions in a more constructive manner. Can you think of all the unnecessary arguments, fights, heartbreaks, and tears you could have saved yourself had you been in slightly better control of your emotions? Emotional intelligence is being considered to be one of the most important aspects of contemporary psychology and with good reason. In addition to this concept being linked to providing greater relationship satisfaction, EQ is also associated with improving your performance at work and in your ability to manage stress in a better way. It is all about making sure that you are in control of your emotions and not the other way round. If you really want to be able to develop deeper and meaningful connections beyond superficial talk with your friends, colleagues, or even your partner, then it would be really helpful if you make developing emotional intelligence as one of your top priorities on your to-do list. But what exactly is EQ all about and how can you improve this?

To put it simply, EQ is all about being able to recognize the emotions you are experiencing, the ability of being able to regulate them while you are empathizing with others and being acutely aware of their reactions as well. It is about balancing the awareness of your own emotions and of those who are around you. When you do this, EQ will help you in managing your relationships in an effective manner even when a conflict emerges. EQ can be developed with practice. The tips mentioned in this section will help you strengthen your relationships by developing your emotional intelligence.

Know yourself: The cornerstone of EQ is self-awareness, and this means that you need to have an understanding of yourself before you try to understand others. If you know yourself well then you will be able to get a more accurate insight into how you come across to others. If you want to increase your self-awareness then you will have to make an effort to focus on your strengths, your triggers, your values, and morals so that you will be able to identify the things that positively make you tick. When you are aware of such things, then the next time around whenever you feel like you might have an emotional outburst you can make a conscious effort of not going down that path.

Strategy for development: Start observing yourself as if you were someone else. Watch what you do and reflect on how you react, how you express yourself and what motivates you. You can go a step further by doing a few tangible exercises to get to know yourself better. You could write your own mock obituary. In it you can define the main components of your life, what your big commitments are, your values and so forth. You could also write a mock dating profile. In it, define your demeanor, what matters to you, what makes you happy or bored. By doing these exercises, you start to observe yourself like others might. You gain a new perspective on how you appear to the outside world and what the fundamentals of your emotional, cognitive and social self are.

Be open to feedback and criticism: You will need to be open to not just feedback but criticism as well. It is highly likely that not everyone will agree with the things that you say or do. You will find it helpful if you can weigh in on the feedback of others before accepting or making any decision. Instead of letting go of your blind spots, you can make use of the feedback you receive to recognize your behaviors that have a negative impact on your life. You need to be able to take criticism constructively. Instead of treating it as a humiliation, you can think of it as an opportunity for learning something new.

Strategy for development: Interview people in your life. This may sound funny when first considering it but trust the process. People in your life love being acknowledged for their wisdom and asked for their opinion, so many will be more than willing to participate. Start by writing down 4-7 questions that you want honest feedback about. For example, 1) What would you say my greatest strengths are? 2) What would you say my greatest weaknesses are? 3) If I were to be more effective in my role [as a dad, mom, employee, president, etc.], what new actions or behaviors should I take? 4) If you could shift one thing about my personality or behavior that would make me more enjoyable to spend time with, what would it be? These are tough questions, and the person may take a few minutes to reflect before answering, but there is so much to be learned through this type of process. Next, think about people in different realms of your life. You may act one way with your family but differently in a social setting or with your work colleagues. Choose 1-3 people from each of your circles and ask them for 10-15 minutes of their time for a one-on-one chat. When you sit down with them, let them know that you are in a process of personal development, that you value their opinion and that you want them to be honest. Take notes of what they say, ask only clarifying questions and do not defend anything. Treat them like they have golden nuggets to share with you and be grateful for anything they say. In the end, it is very normal for the person to want to flip the questioning around and hear what you have to say about them. Offer them the same honesty and do not craft answers based simply on what they said to you. Honor their request too and you will help them develop their emotional intelligence and self- understanding as well.

Identifying your feelings: If you want to develop your emotional intelligence then it will be helpful to start maintaining a journal where you write down things including what's happening around you, your feelings, and the manner in which you reacted to others. Your reaction might have been physical, emotional or even physiological. You can make a list of your roles and feelings you associate with these roles. Think of all the different roles that you play in your life: role of a wife, husband, mother, father, sister, brother, employee, employer, and so on. Think of as many roles as you can and all the different feelings that you associate with these roles. The next thing that you can do is predict how you would feel by thinking about a situation you are in and imagine reacting to another in that situation. You should practice naming and even accepting those feelings. For example, you might feel frustrated, angry, or helpless. When you name these feelings you will have some control over these emotions. Once you are in control of your emotions you will be able to react in an appropriate manner. This exercise will help you in becoming aware of your emotional triggers.

Strategy for development: Write down your emotions as you would name them and then define the physical experience associated with them. Get in touch with how those emotions creep up in your body and are expressed. So if you are experiencing being embarrassed, scan your body and observe how that is physically expressed. Do you feel rumbling in your stomach? Do you feel your shoulders elevate or slight pain in your neck? Do you feel your cheeks get warm and red? This helps build your awareness of your emotions, your feelings and how they physically manifest. You build your awareness. Eventually, you may start being able to simply name the feeling or emotion, observe the physical experience and pay attention to the physical experience and how to handle it, as opposed to following the urge to react. This becomes an exercise in being in the present moment without having to change it. You are simply experiencing it and developing your awareness. You are also becoming more aware of your physical clues as to your emotional state which may help you better identify others physical cues as well.

You will need to be mindful: You will need to make a conscious effort to try and stay mindful in all areas in your life. This means that you will have to start paying close attention to others and stop being judgmental. By learning to observe your thoughts as well as your feelings you will be able to increase your awareness of them, and rather than being bogged down by assumptions you can gain some clarity to think things through. When you are mindful of yourself, the chances of negative emotions overtaking your body are reduced significantly.

Strategy for development: Meditation is a tool used by some of the world's greatest thinkers. It is not just a moment to rest your ever-running brain, but rather an exercise in mind control. The key element of meditation is learning to observe your brain without identifying with it. You learn to watch your emotions and your thoughts without having to grab onto them. You soon see that you are not your thoughts. You are not your emotions. You can simply be a witness to them and choose to engage with them or let them pass like clouds floating by. Our brains are almost always in motion. We are analyzing, considering, reflecting, strategizing, and so forth. When we engage in a practice of meditation, we start taking the reins of our mind. If you have not meditated before or if it has been a while, it helps to start in a quiet space with little distraction. You can set a timer for two or five minutes to start. Use your breath as your center of focus or choose a mental image to focus on. Keep it simple. So once you sit comfortably and start your timer, start to pay attention to your breath. Watch it enter and leave the body. As your mind wanders, which it inevitably will, simply let go of the thought and return to the breath. Many people become frustrated when they start meditating because they feel they are doing it wrong. They will say, "I can't stop thinking. Meditation isn't for me." The fallacy in this statement is that the real exercise of meditation is not the process of turning the brain off. In fact, it is the process of simply letting the thought go when you recognize you have gone down a rabbit hole and return to the centering breath or a centering image in our minds. It is the letting go that is the practice that we hone in meditation but can take forward to all other aspects of our lives. It is us developing our cognitive muscles of being able to identify in our regular lives that we have grabbed onto a thought or emotion that does not empower us, and we can simply let it go. Every time we meditate, we build this capacity within ourselves. So developing a regular practice of even a couple of minutes per day can make a big difference in our ability to be in charge of our own thinking.

Take deep breaths: We tend to experience emotions physically, so when we are stressed out emotionally our bodies tend to have a physical reaction. This results in high levels of blood pressure, cholesterol and so on. None of these are remotely desirable. If you are able to calm down the way your body reacts to stress, then in the same way the emotional component of it can also be tackled successfully. You will need to take steps to nip stress itself in the bud.

When you feel yourself getting tense about something, start taking deep breaths. Concentrate on breathing in and out slowly. This will help you let go of the ball of stress building up within you. When you do this, you will be better equipped at dealing with the emotional situation at hand.

Strategy for development: We often get so wrapped up in being busy and rushing around that we rarely provide ourselves a moment of mental and emotional respite to gather ourselves. Taking a breath is a simple way to slow our bodily processes, ease our minds and give ourselves time to be grounded in the present moment without being consumed by worries or stress. It is helpful to find a cue in your environment to remind you to take a breath. So choose something routine in your life such as stopping at a red light, pumping gas, doing dishes, getting into the shower or something similar. The first few times you start this habit, perhaps you can leave a note to remind yourself. So on your dashboard or on your bathroom mirror, leave a note that says "time to breathe" or "take a breath." Practice three deep breaths when you see this reminder. Eventually, you will match the context with the automatic reminder to take a breath and slow down for a moment. We can all afford 30 seconds to one minute to re- center ourselves. It also helps us bring our emotional state back down to a balanced level so that we can respond more appropriately to what happens in our environment. When we let our stress build without ever releasing it or addressing it, we begin to respond to a fairly mundane circumstance in an exaggerated way. Do yourself a favor and take a moment out of your day to still your mind and calm your emotions and body.

Always question your stories: Never forget that there are multiple ways of viewing the same incident. Instead of letting the negative emotions take you over when you are upset because of someone else's actions, calm down for a minute and take time to analyze the story from the other person's perspective. What might seem deliberate might just be an honest mistake. Let your anger subside before you decide to do something rash and think with a calm and even mind. Question the stories you think happened even if you believe they are true. Looking at an incident from the perspective of a neutral third party can definitely change your perspective.

Strategy for development: Think of an event that still bothers you in some way. Take a piece of paper and draw a vertical line down the middle. At the top of the left column, write "What happened" and at the top of the right column write "Story, what I added." We always naturally build a story around things that happen. We come up with the "whys" and the reasons. Without having to put much conscious effort in at all, we develop a whole notion about the other person's motivations and so on. This exercise is one about learning to differentiate reality from all the things we automatically add which is the story or the untruth. Now this isn't to say that your assumptions may be incorrect or that the other person is always acting in good faith. This may not be the case. But when we build stories without identifying that we have actually created them in our minds, we miss the opportunity to be conscious and leave space to see the situation in more than just one way. The real goal here is to find an empowering context. So, if you take the example that someone at work 'didn't appreciate your work', start looking at what actually happened. So in the left column, write verbatim what was said. Don't write things like 'they talked down to me and tried to make me feel stupid.' Instead, write 'At the staff meeting 2 weeks ago, John said "we have to take a new direction with this project."' Remember, this column is for things that actually happened in reality and could be witnessed by anyone watching (so not interpreted or assumed). Then in the right column, write all of the judgments, assessments, and ideas that you added. What did you make that statement or the action the other person took mean? As you go through this process, you quickly see how much we each add to something. We apply our own filters, we bring our own history to it, and we judge. If everyone were to do this exercise, we would find that some things may be common, but everyone tends to add their own notions to what happens externally. That is where we gain a better understanding of how we are each responsible for our own opinions. We create them. We often don't consciously construct them, but they are our own. Our brains fill in the blanks, and suddenly we think our opinions are what happened in reality. The next step is to consider how others involved in the scenario might apply their own filters and judgments. From their perspective, how did they see the circumstance? You could journal as if you were them. Write about what happened, how you felt, what worried you, how you interpreted the situation, and what you want to happen next. Developing this type of empathy will likely open a new door for you to be more understanding of others but also to be more literate of your and other people's mental processes.

Chapter 8:

Emotional Intelligence in Social Situations

Establishing social ties is important for human beings, and emotional intelligence plays an important role in this establishment. To increase your social presence, it's vital to use your emotional intelligence. It will improve your overall development. This relates to the way you interact with others and has a direct bearing on the way they interact with you.

While we looked at workplace situations in the previous chapter, this chapter will focus on how to use your emotional intelligence wisely in social situations. It will help you to shine as a human being if you can use the information in this chapter to help your relationships because you will be opening yourself up to new possibilities.

Speak freely

You can't always think too much and worry too much about the things you are about to say. This can have a lot of negative impact on your emotional health. You need to speak freely and without fear in order to win friends and allies.

If you overthink things before saying them, you won't be able to make lasting relationships. Communication is very important in a relationship, so you must be able to convey your feelings freely without the fear of being judged. Keep in mind that you won't be judged for the things you say if you say them confidently. Acting unsure, however, will make others doubt you and harm your credibility. Trust is important in a friendship, so speak as freely as possible.

While this is said to be great for your relationships, bear in mind that as you change the way that you think, you will be less thoughtless in your comments and will make an attempt to be more empathetic toward your social circle of friends. Test yourself on this and write down things that have created a bad reaction. Then look at what happened in those circumstances so you can work out a better way of approaching that topic in the future. The thing you need to keep in mind is that no matter how honest you are in your communication with others, there will be times when you say the wrong thing at the wrong time. Not because you are being less than honest, but because the person you are talking to isn't as receptive as you wish they were. You can't dictate the way that other people feel, but once you realize that they are feeling down or that they have problems, you can use your emotional intelligence to help them out of the doldrums and back to feeling good about themselves.

People who are open and honest and who are able to speak freely will also pick up on moods of others and be able to gauge their conversation to suit the occasion. People without emotional intelligence don't distinguish and often blame others when there are disagreements. You need to be assertive, but not to the extent that you make fun of others or belittle them. Once you pick up on their bad situation, you are also the first there to try and assist them and that's why people like you. You don't proffer advice in such a way that it feels like you are trying to overload someone with your own feelings. Emotionally intelligent people are able to adjust their conversation to take into account things others may not even notice.

Listen

I cannot stress enough the importance of listening. It is so important that you carefully listen to others. There needs to be a balance between how much you say and how much you listen. You can't always expect people to listen to you without you listening to them. If you don't listen to others, they won't be interested in hearing what you say either. How often do you notice people asking how you are and then walking away before you have a chance to answer? This is a common occurrence and shows a total lack of empathy toward the other person. Although it may be politically correct to ask people how they are, emotionally intelligent people actually wait for the recipient of the question to answer because they care sufficiently to listen.

Listening is also necessary for you because it keeps your thoughts and emotions in check. If you don't listen to anyone else, you will develop irrational thoughts or emotions, and acting on them will result in problems. Listening to others helps establish easy communication between people. It also makes you a great friend to have. If you have people within your social circle who are unhappy, listening to them gives you clues so you can help them to understand that much of their unhappiness is happening because of their response to some stimuli. You need to pass on the knowledge that not everyone sees things in the same way as the person who offended them, but that they need to be thick-skinned when it comes to allowing others to get inside their heads.

Establish understanding

Empathy and understanding are a huge part of social intelligence, and you must be good at both to sit well in a group. Friendships can only last when there is some emotional intelligence at play. If that's not the case, the two people involved won't be able to communicate very effectively and this miscommunication will result in problems. This is why people with low emotional intelligence are encouraged to put efforts into improving their emotional intelligence. The next time that you have a conversation with a friend, try to pick up on their mood. Try to listen to what they say and then try to place yourself in their situation before you come up with solutions. This involves empathy and practice of empathy is something that people with great emotional intelligence are very good at.

If you listen to a conversation and watch who dominates the conversation, these are usually people who think more of themselves than they do of their audience. These are the bores in life that offer little empathy and don't really listen or try to understand others because they feel they are self-sufficient. In actuality, they are tactless and probably have major issues in their lives of their own causing. They may not realize they are not listening to people and will certainly be shocked if you were to suggest that. Learn from watching because you will instantly recognize those with low emotional intelligence levels.

One thing that you will notice are those people who have adapted to their high emotional intelligence levels because these are the people who stand out in a crowd and who everyone wants as their friend.

Making new friends

To be successful, you need a decent network of people, and to establish this network, you need to be able to use your social intelligence well. This will help you win over new people, especially influential ones, and add new friends to your social circle. This is really important if you want to progress in life. When you have better connections, it increases your chances of better job opportunities and making it big in your field of interest.

When you make new friends, remember to use your emotional intelligence to foster a great relationship. That doesn't mean being as clever — or even cleverer — than the new friend. It's not a question of one-upmanship. It's a matter of being yourself and being aware that your new friend is worth getting to know as well. You don't need to impress. You need to listen, to learn, and to use your emotional intelligence to know when it's appropriate to listen and when it's appropriate to speak. Generally, those with high emotional intelligence recognize this instantly, though if you are new to using your emotional intelligence, take each conversation as it comes and never be jealous of someone else in the spotlight. Your emotional intelligence means you have the common sense to know there are no real stars. There are just people and the more a new friend talks, the more you get an opportunity to learn about him or her, which is a very good thing.

Maintaining existing ties

I have often heard people say that friendships don't last and that it is all meant to fade away with time. That is not true at all and you shouldn't take this as practical advice. Maintaining ties is always good for you and it's very possible when you use your emotional intelligence and realize that a certain amount of give and take is required to keep a relationship alive. Yes, there will be changes in the relationship dynamics as the time passes, and your emotions will change, but you can keep adapting to the new situations as long as you don't give up and let irrational thoughts into your head.

For example, if a friend moves away, you should be receptive enough to know that not only are you feeling the absence, they are as well. An extra phone call to your friend when he or she is settling into a new environment will always be welcome. Keeping in touch means keeping them in your social circle even if you are absent from each other. With social networking, Skype, and email, there's no reason to cut a person out of your life just because he or she lives in another town. Keeping yourself in touch shows a great deal of emotional intelligence because you are making yourself available to a wider audience of friends and helping the relationship last for a longer time.

These are some of the things you must keep in mind when making use of your emotional intelligence in social situations.

Chapter 9:

Tips to Increase your Emotional Intelligence

Dealing with Negative Emotions

A rguably, the most important aspect of emotional intelligence is your ability to deal with your negative emotions. Managing emotions so they don't overwhelm you and cloud your judgment is incredibly important. To change the way you feel about a situation, you first must change how you *think* about it. Let's take a look at some examples:

A. **Negative Personalization:** It's common for us to feel unfavorably towards someone and their behavior, and this may lead us to jump to conclusions, so it's important that we don't. Instead, we should try to view the situation differently. Try to come up with different angles before you react. Take the example of a friend who didn't return your call. You may be tempted to think that he or she is ignoring you, but take a moment to think about the entire situation. There's no reason your friend should start ignoring you without cause. He or she might just be busy. You will only consider that when you avoid personalizing people's behavior. Everyone does their own thing for *themselves* more than thinking about how their behavior affects other people. So it's important you widen your perspective in order to reduce misunderstanding. You don't know what's happening with your absent friend and assuming that you do is not exercising emotional intelligence at all. The better way forward would be to break the ice at the first opportunity you get by telephoning your friend. You may find you prolong your friendship and that your friend may have thought it was *you* who had lost interest in him or her.

B. **Fear of Rejection:** Always provide yourself with more than one option in an important situation. This helps ensure that you will have strong alternatives in case one plan fails. It's a really effective way to manage your fear of rejection. I'm sure you've heard this expression, but never put all of your eggs in one basket. If you depend on one person to such an extent that you will suffer bad disappointment if you are let down, you are opening yourself up to hurt. Now, you can also apply this to emotions. Think of a Plan B and even a Plan C when you are approaching a situation. Don't assume the worst when your date doesn't turn up. Simply do something yourself and wait for their explanation. It may actually be something quite innocent that stopped that person from turning up, but you will never know if you accuse them of letting you down before first listening to an explanation. Learn to be intelligent and not so needy of others. Yes, it was inconsiderate for him or her not to turn up, but things happen that are beyond people's control and sometimes you have to accept that plans change.

Here's an example: You are applying for an amazing job and you're really excited. If you tell yourself you'll be devastated if don't hire you, your fear of rejection will cripple you. Instead, plan to apply for more than one job. Then tell yourself, "There are three fantastic jobs I'll be applying for. I'm definitely going to be well-qualified for one or more!" It's like seeing the cup half full as opposed to seeing it as half empty. If you view life in this way, you are actually being more emotionally intelligent than you think because you are setting yourself up for success. If you do the opposite and set yourself up for failure, one thing is sure: you will undoubtedly fail.

Staying Cool and Managing Stress

Experiencing some degree of stress is commonplace for most of us. What makes the difference for us is how we choose to deal with stressful situations. Handing stress well can mean all the difference between being reactive and being assertive, between being frazzled and being poised. Always keep your cool when under pressure. Here are two tips to do that:

A. Whenever you're nervous or angry, wash your face with some cold water and then go out to take in some fresh air. Cooling down the temperature around you will help reduce your anxiety. Remember to stay away from caffeine because it stimulates nervousness. Another way to deal with this is to simply go out in the fresh air and breathe slowly and purposefully in order to level out the oxygen in your body. When people are stressed they tend to hyperventilate. If you know yourself well and know that you do this, then the fresh air and calm breathing will help you to get things back into perspective.

B. Whenever you're depressed, discouraged or fearful, go to the gym for some intense aerobic exercises. This will energize your body and mind and make you feel much better. Motion dictates emotion, as the saying goes. So whenever you need to feel more confident, exercise and experience your body's vitality. This will get your adrenalin pumping, which may be all that you need to actually get through the situation in a way that energizes you instead of zapping your energy.

Being Assertive and Expressing Difficult Emotions

"Being who we are requires that we can talk openly about things that are important to us, that we take a clear position on where we stand on important emotional issues, and that we clarify the limits of what is acceptable and tolerable to us in a relationship."

— Harriet Lerner

We often face situations in our lives when we have to set our boundaries in order to let people know where we stand. There are many situations where it's important that you stay assertive and get your point across. You have the right to disagree without being offensive, decline a request without feeling guilty, set your own priorities, and protect yourself from duress or harm. This is all part and parcel of being a grown up human being. You need to recognize those times when you need to make the right choices.

When dealing with difficult emotions, it's easy to get overwhelmed. But there's one method that I find works well for me when trying to express difficult emotions — the XYZ technique. It can be explained in one simple sentence: I feel X when you do Y in situation Z.

Take a look at some examples:

"I feel disappointed that you didn't come through for me when you promised you would."

"I feel horrified that the government isn't giving him proper recognition when he has done so much for the country."

Did you notice something in the sentence formation? It shifts the focus of the statement to the speaker, thereby making it more acceptable. One must avoid using statements that begin with "you," as they are most often followed by a judgement or accusation. This almost always puts the listener on the defensive. Sentences like that will make your audience much less likely to listen to what you have to say or the reasoning you have to offer, however compelling it may be. You have to remember that even emotionally intelligent people won't respond to this kind of accusatory statement. It's better to reword what you say so that they know that your statement is not specifically aimed at them. You can explain things and, if you use your emotional intelligence to put forward ideas, you will also find that you are able to do so without offending anyone at all.

Staying Proactive When Faced With a Difficult Person

There are a lot of unreasonable people out there, and you are bound to encounter one at some point of time. You could be stuck with someone like that at work, or even at home, and it's easy for such people to ruin our day if we let them. To handle such difficult people, you need to stay proactive. Here are some tips:

A. Take a deep breath and slowly count to ten whenever you feel angry or upset with someone. This makes sure that you won't say anything you might regret later. Nine out of ten times, you would already have calmed down and figured out a way to deal with the situation in a better manner by the time you finish counting. This will reduce the problem instead of further aggravating it. If you're still upset over the problem, take time out and revisit it later when you have calmed down. If you approach any topic when you are feeling mad, you are not actually using your emotional intelligence. I can give you a good example here. Unfortunately, once a year, I have to endure having relatives stay at my house. There are two who are particularly offensive and I learned when I was younger that if I took their bait as they expected me to, I was actually feeding into their nastiness. Instead of doing that, I simply told myself that they were guests and that after they had gone, I could easily adjust back to my simple way of living and not let them affect me or the way that I felt. It was actually much easier than you might imagine. If they wound me up, I simply laughed. If they tried to get an angry reaction from me, I didn't engage. Instead, I was the perfect host and they had no reason to continue their obnoxious behavior because they were not getting their desired effect.

B. You don't want to be reactive; you want to be proactive. So, just for a moment, try to put yourself in the other person's shoes. It's difficult, but it will give you some perspective.

Consider the other person and their situation, and then tell yourself how it must be hard to be in that situation. For example, read this sentence:

"My mother is being so moody. It must not be easy dealing with so many responsibilities and so much stress."

This is not to say these situations excuse bad behavior. It's just to remind you, everyone has their own issues and that is why they do what they do. Be reasonable and considerate to others. Remind yourself the behavior of others tells a lot more about them than anyone else around them can, including us. This helps you in objectively viewing the situation and in coming up with good solutions.

C. Identifying and asserting consequences is important when you want the other person to stand down. This ability can save you a lot of trouble when dealing with a difficult person. If you articulate yourself effectively enough, you can cause the person to stop and consider the situation for a moment, keeping in mind the consequences. You cannot do this effectively if you are on the defensive. However, if you can use emotional intelligence, you will be able to see their behavior from another perspective.

Bouncing Back from Adversity

Did you know that Michael Jordan — yes, the one and only — has missed over 9,000 shots in his career, and that he has lost almost 300 games? He has missed winning shots when he was trusted to take those shots. But the great thing is he has gotten back up each time he failed or got knocked down. That is why he is so successful.

It's important to realize that you won't always get what you want, and that life can be hard at times. Life often presents us with challenges, and how we choose to deal with them makes all the difference. You can be hopeful or you can despair, you can be optimistic or you can feel frustrated, all of which will affect how you approach situations. Try thinking of that cup, half full, when you have a situation where you have to make a decision or a move. Think of the overall situation. See it from both your own perspective and the other person's perspective. This makes you much more in control than you can ever be from only seeing your side of the coin.

No matter how the situation resolves, you must ask yourself if you learned anything from the experience and know that what lies ahead is more important now. Ask yourself good questions and you will get high quality answers that help you prioritize better and learn to live a full life. You will gain perspective and tackle future situations in much better ways.

One of the best parts of my training as a Samaritan was that I needed to put my own judgement to one side and listen to what someone was saying. In this type of work, what you are doing is dealing with life and death situations where people's emotions are at such a low that saying the wrong thing can push them over the edge. I started to use this technique in relationships in general and found it gave me a much wider view of the problem. I first took my own emotions out of the equation because they don't help me to deal with the problem at hand. With difficult situations, if you can learn to let this part of your mind switch off and look at the logic of the situation, rather than seeing something to criticize, you will be able to help the person with difficulties overcome them. Then you can decide if this person is still your friend. While a situation is critical, you need to separate out what you are thinking because of your experiences and sentiments and what common sense you can make of the situation. Let the common sense side of you in to help solve the problem. There are times when emotions get in the way and someone with emotional intelligence will know when it's time to use logic rather than emotions.

Expressing Intimate Emotions in Personal Relationships

Showing love and affection is vital in every close relationship. Your ability to effectively express these emotions and validate them plays a big part in how your personal relationships play out. "Effective" here means that you share feelings with the other person in a constructive, nourishing, and affirmative matter, thus showing another you receive their feelings and reciprocate. Never be afraid of letting down your barriers when it comes to intimate relationships. People who are free in their emotional relationships and who are able to show appreciation and love will always have better relationships than those who hold back.

Any method of positive connection that people use to express intimate emotions in relationships is called "bidding," according to Dr. John Gottman. Positive eye contact and gestures like smiling, hugging, and putting an arm around someone's shoulder can be seen as body language "bidding." Verbally telling others how you feel about them is "verbal bidding." There's another type as well, "behavioral bidding." When you offer someone food, give them a thoughtful gift, or do them a favor, it's all part of "behavioral bidding." All these things create a closer bond between you and another person.

A research study shows that in healthy relationships, people can bid with each other hundreds of times, both in small and large ways, during the course of a day. The essence is to convey to the other person, "I care about you and want to stay connected with you." It's crucial for any relationship to have constant and consistent bidding between the involved parties.

If you are in a relationship and feel that the relationship is going stale, then you need to examine both sides of the relationship. It may not be your partner who is at fault. It may be that you are not bidding anymore and that they are not reciprocating because they are too afraid to and do not want to feel that awful feeling of rejection.

The ways that people do this may be simple, but those with emotional intelligence will make their partner feel loved and wanted with even the smallest of gestures. These acts are likely to help sustain a very strong relationship. Here are some affirmative actions that you can take to show your partner that he or she means a great deal to you:

Give your partner his/her favorite flowers
Wear a provocative scent and ask your partner for
appreciation
Make a cup of coffee for your
loved one and offer a heart
shaped biscuit with it Offer your
partner a spoonful of a delicious
dessert
Ask your partner
to scratch your
back and show
appreciation Tell
your partner how
much you love
him/her

- Choose intimate moments to be together and share
- Remind them of your favorite song or favorite memory together

Often when a relationship has been going on for a long time, we forget the importance of these promises, though they mean every bit as much twenty years into a relationship as they do in the first six months. You are affirming your love. Emotionally mature people are not afraid to do that, whereas those with emotional problems may find they don't show feelings and then blame their partner for not showing emotions. It's very much a two-way thing and if you have been neglecting your close relationship it's not too late to pull it all back together by using your emotional intelligence to strengthen the relationship and put it back onto the pedestal it once used to be placed upon. Love is a very valuable emotion that should never be neglected. If you look at what you consider to be ideal relationships among your friends, you will find that the language of love isn't something that has stopped just because the couple has been together for a long time. Emotionally intelligent people know that kindling love and keeping the flame alight is very important. It may be a good time to bring out those old photographs and reminisce together about your early days to remind you both of what you once had and then work together to bring back those feelings by showing your emotions and not being afraid to say, "I love you."

What emotionally intelligent people realize is that life is not going to go on forever. If they leave these thoughts unspoken, they may never have a chance to say what they mean. Thus they will maximize on showing affection to loved ones. Having time together and listening is also very important as your loved one may have needs that you haven't even considered. When you listen, you can evolve with the relationship and adjust your emotional response to fit any existing situation, thus letting your loved one know that even though things have changed, your love remains a constant in your lives.

Chapter 10:

Everyday Communication Skills

B y now, you must have realized that communication is an important part of emotional intelligence, so you have to have great communication skills in order to display a high level of emotional intelligence. In this chapter, we will take a look at some very important verbal and nonverbal communication skills you should ensure are ever-present in your life.

Making Conversation

Some people are naturally good at making conversation while others struggle even with simple small talk. If someone suffers from social anxiety, even the idea of small talk can make him or her nervous or terrified. Regardless, there are some things that can help everyone make more meaningful and comfortable conversations to build healthy relationships.

Identifying Troubled Areas

Almost all of us have some troubled areas when it comes to communicating effectively. The first thing you must do is identify them. Take a look at your daily social interactions and think about times you face problems. Ask yourself questions to help you identify the problems and decide what is the best course of action to correct them. You can start by asking yourself simple questions like "Do I talk too much?" "Do I struggle with breaking the ice?" "Do I feel uncomfortable expressing my opinions?"

Once you do that and work towards fixing the issues, you will feel more confident. You can also establish what you are doing wrong by listening more and hearing what friends have to say. There may be difficult situations arising because you don't listen enough and thus don't understand the nuances of the relationship and can't see what is coming or why. When you listen, you are able to understand so much more and this helps you to level out your anxiety and communicate in a much more effective manner.

Starting a Conversation

Starting a conversation with a stranger can be really difficult, so you don't need to talk about very specific things. You can start off by saying really general things, like "This party is really nice, right?" You can also compliment the weather, as cliché as it sounds. Other things you can do is make unassuming observations about the other person or tell them a little something about yourself. All of it works as long as you don't try too hard to sound clever or funny. If you come up with something spontaneously, go for it. If you don't, that's fine too; don't feel compelled to be witty. Politeness and sincerity matter the most in a conversation. As a good introduction to new people, look for common ground. If you are introduced to someone at a party, listen first, and when you find a mutual interest your communication will be easier.

If you already know the person a little, you can also discuss slightly more personal topics. Be natural and be yourself but always remember that emotionally intelligent people allow whomever they are getting to know lots of leeway when it comes to talking about them. Once you have broken the ice and found things that you have in common, the rest is really easy. You also have to remember that the person you are making friends with may be just as anxious as you are. If you do notice that, try to put them at ease. Typical statements that can be made which will help are:

"I see you are just as nervous as me about meeting people." "I don't know many people here, do you?"
"A penny for your thoughts?"

Each of these encourages the person to feel more comfortable in your presence and emotional intelligence should do the rest. Be open to listening to what they have to say and let the relationship follow its normal course. However, don't try too hard to be something that you are not. There is absolutely no emotional intelligence at play when you do that because you are setting yourself up for failure.

Keeping it going

For some people, starting a conversation comes pretty easily, but keeping it going is the bane of their existence. The key thing to remember is you are only one half of the conversation, so you don't need to put in all of the effort. There are a lot of ways to easily keep a conversation going:

> Pay attention to the things the other person says without giving the impression that they're the only one who's talking. Try and contribute to the conversation. Use the right body language to show that you are listening attentively to what they have to say.

> There are so many things you can easily talk about: TV shows, movies, hobbies, weekend plans, and study courses, among other subjects. What you talk about doesn't matter much as long as you keep it going comfortably.

> Avoid asking personal questions when you are just beginning to know a person. Put yourself in

their position and consider whether you'll like it if someone asked you the same kind of question. Keep the conversation light and interesting, and tell the person something about yourself.

- Open-ended questions work really well. They allow room for much better responses and longer conversations. Plus, they open up conversations that can end up going in all kinds of interesting directions.

- Maintaining good eye contact and smiling wherever necessary is good for a conversation. It keeps the other person interested and shows that you are feeling positive towards the conversation.

- Discuss things like books, restaurants, and other things and ask the other person their opinions on those subjects. It gives you a window into their mind and also gives you opportunity to find more topics of conversation.

Ending a Conversation

It is inevitable that a conversation will come to an end. Accept this and be comfortable with it. When you feel like the end is near, don't try to prolong the conversation unnecessarily. People who are new to each other usually don't have very long conversations anyway. It's good to keep the conversation light and moderately long in such a situation. Remember, emotional intelligence is your guide and you should listen to what your mind is telling you about the conversation. Sometimes, letting go is the biggest lure to the other person to contact you again in the future. People who don't exercise emotional intelligence tend to be the last ones to leave the party, but are often the first people others want to forget. They are too needy and put their needs above the comfort levels of people around them.

You don't have to feel like a failure when the conversation is coming to an end. Rather, you should put in some effort into ending it smoothly. You can ask the other about future plans, like coffee or lunch. You can also tell them that it was great seeing them and that you need to catch up with someone or something else now. If you end the conversation in a smooth manner, you both will have something to look forward to for your next conversation, and nobody will feel awkward. Emotional intelligence allows you to know when it's time to call it quits for the time being.

Practice and Experimentation

This may sound weird to some of you, but practicing and experimenting can really make a difference when you have a real live conversation. Stand in front of a mirror and say some opening lines to yourself so you know how you sound.

You can also record yourself to hear yourself, which will help you identify what needs to be fixed, if anything. You need to see what message you are conveying emotionally to another person, so act normally in front of the mirror and observe honestly. That will help you to see where you are failing in using emotional intelligence.

Another thing you can do is experiment while having a real conversation. Break your normal patterns every now and then, and go a little out of your comfort zone. Try letting the other person close a conversation if you are the one who does it most of the times. Talk to a stranger every once in a while, or invite your neighbor to lunch. Sit with a coworker you seldom talk to, and ask them for coffee. Give someone a small compliment, and remember to do it sincerely. These little things make a lot of difference. What they are doing is allowing you to practice your emotional intelligence and helping you to be able to read people better than you do at the moment. In fact, the wider the range of people that you communicate with, the more you learn about the way that people respond. You also learn about weaknesses, facial expressions, and the way people handle their emotions.

Nonverbal Communication

Did you know that most of what we communicate is actually done through nonverbal cues? Seems odd, or even surprising, right? But it's true. What you convey with your expressions, your body language, and your tone tells a story in and of itself. Sometimes, the story can be even more compelling than the words you are actually saying. These gestures and cues send strong messages to others. They tell about your state of mind, your attitude, knowledge, and even motives, among other things. So you have to pay attention to what you are conveying nonverbally, too. Your gestures should be in sync with your verbal communication.

Do an exercise in observation because this will give you a great opportunity to test out your emotional intelligence. Are you picking up the right vibes? Are you able to get inside someone else's skin? Are you able to empathize? All of these skills help you to be able to read people in a more efficient way and to communicate more effectively.

Identifying Trouble Areas

Try and always be aware of your eye contact, posture, volume, tone, expressions and gestures. Along with that, also pay attention to the distance between you and the other person. Ask yourself some of these questions:

Am I maintaining eye contact?

Do I feel comfortable maintaining eye contact? Am I smiling enough?
Am I sitting up straight?

- Is the other person hearing me properly at this
- volume? Do I sound too cocky or anxious?
- Am I crossing my arms or legs?

At the same time that you are asking yourself these questions, you are also learning about people's gestures and will be able to ask yourself:

Is he/she maintaining eye contact? Is he/she comfortable with me?
What does his smile tell me about him? Why is he slouching?
Does he understand what I am trying to say? Is he even interested in my conversation?
Does he act in a cocky manner?
What does his body language tell me about him?

You can see it's always about two-way communication. Your body language is every bit as important as the other person's body language. It also lets you know the following:

Does he have a complex?
Does he have self-esteem issues? How would I feel in his place?
What are his eyes telling me about what he is thinking? What is his body language telling me that he isn't?

There are so many questions that come up that are relevant to communication. The more you can observe and learn from conversations, the more able you will be to exercise your emotional intelligence. You will know from reactions the effect that your conversation is having and that's very important knowledge in any kind of relationship — be it in the work environment, in interviews or simply with meeting someone for the very first time.

Practice and Experimentation

Your nonverbal skills are as important as your verbal skills, if not more, so make sure you take the time to practice and experiment with them. Practice in front of the mirror and pay close attention. If possible, ask a friend or a family member to give you honest feedback on what you need to work on. Try new things when talking to strangers and see how they respond. Positive reactions are affirmation that you're doing something right. All you need to do is pay attention and be conscious in the moment. Slowly, things will start coming naturally to you. Try a smile at the right moment and see what response you get because you will find different kinds of smiles lead to different reactions. You need to experiment with people.

Here's an exercise: ask a good friend to read your expressions. Now, think of an adjective such as sad and act out that adjective with your body language. See if your friend is emotionally intelligent enough to pick up on it. Then get them to do the same so that you get the same practice and are able to distinguish what they are feeling simply from how they look and what their body is saying.

Assertiveness

Before we start, let's make sure you don't mistake assertiveness for aggressiveness. Many people make this mistake, and as a result, stay away from assertive communication. This is not true, however, as being assertive is totally different from being passive or aggressive. You can voice your opinions strongly and honestly without being judgemental or threatening to anyone around you. It is really the best way you can communicate, but it takes time and effort to master, especially for people who have social anxiety.

Some people are so hell-bent on avoiding conflict that they tend to agree with everyone, even if their own opinions and feelings conflict with it. The idea of opposing someone's opinion is scary to some people, and they don't do it in fear of offending or hurting the other person. This is really bad for good communication though. If you are in a situation and you are asked what you think about something, try looking inward and using your emotional intelligence to answer the question instead of fretting about what the reaction will be. If you are earnest in your opinion, regardless of whether others agree with it, they will respect your right to have your own set of values.

To be good at communication and build a solid social network, you have to take charge of your life and start being assertive. When you feel something, let it be known in a non-threatening manner. Remember that you are allowed to say "no" if you are unable or unwilling to fulfill someone's demands. Your right to do that is respected and you do not have to ever feel guilty about it.

Try this on social networking sites. This exercise really helps because even the most timid of people can actually show their true colors in replies to questions that are posed on websites. You need to remember that an emotionally intelligent person will never purposefully do anyone harm because they know that's not an intelligent thing to do. What you learn from social networking websites is how to correspond with others and show that you actually care about something. Sometimes, you can see a posting from someone about illness on websites and if you look at the set of replies, you will notice a lot of people will reply in a very generic way. There will be smileys, hearts, people offering prayers, etc. but because these are so common, they have little value. They are almost like the person asking how you are and then turning away before you answer. Stand out from the crowd by using your emotional intelligence to stand out as someone who is very humane and sincere.

The amount of people that folk have as friends on websites such as these is something that is relatively meaningless.

However, in real life, it does matter how many friends you have and may make a difference on your level of happiness. Therefore, don't waste time chasing up friendships on social networking sites. Instead, try and concentrate your efforts into building real life relationships that will become a part of your everyday life. Learn from social networking sites and using them as a forum in which you can practice your emotional intelligence.

The more you step back and use your emotional intelligence, the better able you will be to make friends and to influence people, because people will use you as their example of how they want to be. If you are the person who can keep his/her cool in bad situations, others will want to be like you. Your emotional intelligence should lead you to being able to cope with just about anything. The way that you deal with things always involves the following:

- Listening Empathizing
- Finding solutions without being judgemental
- Pleasing others by pleasing yourself

However, if you don't have a very high level of emotional intelligence you can mistake the last one in that list and offend people. Emotionally intelligent people know the difference between pleasing themselves at the expense of others and doing so within acceptable boundaries.

Chapter 11:

People Skills

Interpersonal skills, also known as people skills or soft skills, are your abilities to interact well with other people. It includes your knowledge of basic psychology and social interaction. It's much more than some people make it out to be. Having strong interpersonal skills is not simply having a good personality or being likeable. That's only the surface, one aspect of it you can see. There's so much more to it as you are about to find out.

Your people skills help you in your personal relationships as well as in your professional relationships. You have to demonstrate these skills well if you want to be successful and happy in life.

Trust and Honesty

Trust is really important among peers to achieve collective goals and maintain fruitful relationships. If there is no trust between you and your coworkers, or between you and your friends, your relationships will be baseless and have no real use to you or to others. To find solutions to problems together, you need to trust and cooperate with each other. What you need first and foremost is trust. To inculcate it in your personality, you can do various trust building exercises.

Strategy for development: One fun exercise is the minefield. If you have never done this with colleagues and friends, then perhaps it's time that you tried. One of you is blindfolded and chooses someone who they trust to guide them through the minefield. The minefield is made up of obstacles. Total trust is needed for this to work well and by exercising total control over the situation, you win trust. Try it with someone who doesn't trust you, but make sure that every instruction you give is concise. Make sure there are no mistaken moves because this won't win you trust. This is a good team building exercise, and when used in the workplace can help people to bond in such a way that they learn to trust the instincts of their colleagues.

Trust-falls are also a good exercise to establish trust. Two people stand together, both facing the same way. The person in front is to trust the person behind and fall in a completely relaxed fashion into the arms of the person behind, trusting that they will catch them and that they are safe. This is also done in group environments and is a useful tool for creating trust.

Honesty is another important thing you need. It is the bedrock of any relationship. Trust requires honesty, and the people involved need to be transparent with each other in all their dealings. It is a very delicate thread, and once lost, trust is very difficult to get back. "Honesty is the best policy" is not something you just throw around; you need to stick to it. There are ways to deal with awkward situations where your honesty is asked for, but an honest answer may hurt others. People with emotional intelligence won't need to think twice about answering. They will be able to answer without hurting the recipient of that answer. An example of this:

"Do you think this style of dress suits me?"

In actual fact it looks absolutely terrible, but the idea is not to hurt the person who asked. Someone with emotional intelligence would simply pass another dress to the individual and say,

"I think you will find this style is more flattering."

What they are doing is being truthful without hurting the person who asked their advice, but they are also proffering an alternative. That is a great way to deal with situations such as this. Not only are they being honest, but they are exercising caution in the way that they handle the situation.

Patience

All of us are not born the same. We possess different degrees of proficiency in different tasks, and you can't expect the same level of competence from everyone in everything. Some people might be good at one thing while some might be good at another. So when you want someone to do something for you, you need to be patient. It's easy to lose patience in a stressful situation, but expressing impatience can sometimes be really bad. Try to maintain your cool for as long as possible and you will maintain strong relationships.

You will notice that people who have high emotional intelligence will devise teaching methods so others learn without too much difficulty. They are patient, but the emotional intelligence they have leads them to find ways that relate to the person being taught, so that they can easily learn.

An example of this is a child who found math difficult. He cannot see the figures or if he does, they mean nothing to

him. The same lesson can be taught using marbles, making the lesson more relevant to the child. It will be the emotional intelligence that kicks in and allows the teacher to adjust to fit the given situation.

Strategy for development: Think of a situation where you normally find yourself wanting to rush or perhaps you experience frustration. A good example may be driving in traffic or waiting in line. Put yourself in one of those situations where you normally experience impatience rearing its head. In this situation, simply observe what is happening. See if others around you are displaying signs of being impatient. Take your time just watching, smiling and breathing. Remind yourself that there is nowhere else to be at that moment. Listen and watch what happens in your body as you feel the urge to want to change things, for things to be different, faster, etc. Just observe. The process of just being an observer and suspending the urge to take action is you developing your ability to be patient. It is you stopping your fight with the way things are and accepting the present moment as it is. This doesn't mean that you are meant to be a bump on a log and just let life happen to you. Eventually, as you develop patience, you learn the process of observing, looking for solutions and acting appropriately. Not reacting. However, in your initial stages of just learning patience, simply focus on being still and staying present to what is happening without having to do something about it.

Empathy

Sometimes, you may feel the need to lash out at someone when they do something you find offensive or act in a way you don't like. It's easy to give in to this, but you need to stay calm and empathize with that person. Try and see things from his or her perspective and you might realize there's no need to react so strongly. Understanding another person's point of view and situation is really important. It is not the same as agreeing to what they say or do, but even if you disagree, you can choose to do it with courtesy. It's more about understanding than agreeing.

The other thing is that empathy allows you to step back and give ownership for the bad behavior to the person who has committed it. If you disagree with something that someone does, instead of chastising them for their behavior, thank your lucky stars you don't have to resort to such behavior because your circumstances allow you to find an alternative.

Strategy for development: When you are in a situation where someone is reacting to something, in a calm way simply acknowledge their experience. So you might say, "I understand it is frustrating that you have not heard back from your boss about getting the vacation time you requested. I'm sorry you are still waiting." So you are not agreeing with them or condoning their behavior, but you are observing and acknowledging what that experience is like for them. They might correct you and clarify how they are actually feeling. Just be with them and listen to what they have to say. Let your only goal be that of empathizing with them, wherever they are at. Even if they are reacting in a way that makes no sense from your perspective, that is not the point of the exercise. Empathy is being able to see it from their perspective. They are the focus and what is important.

You may find that by letting them know they have been heard, it dissipates their negative experience. Sometimes people act out because they don't feel like they are heard, so by giving them attention and showing care towards them, they might lose that motivation to act out and instead might find a new approach to their situation.

Active Listening

If you are the kind of person who starts framing a reply as soon as the other person starts speaking, you're doing it wrong. We are given two ears for a reason. As I have said before, really listen to the other person and understand what they are saying, because it is as important as what you are saying. In fact, people who use emotional intelligence will appreciate that what other people are saying is actually probably more important. Active listening takes effort and patience, but it pays off in the long run. Don't interrupt the other person when he or she is speaking. Let the other person finish; understand what he or she said, and then form an appropriate response. That's the intelligent way because you are letting your head rule rather than your emotions.

Strategy for development: Firstly, when someone comes to speak with you, give your full indication that you intend to listen to them. Even say, "let me just finish this text, then turn off my phone so I can give you my full attention." Then practice making eye contact. When they take a pause from speaking, reframe what they are saying and ask if you are hearing them correctly. So if your child is telling you about someone who made fun of them at school, you might say "so when you were in the cafeteria today, Jennifer said that your clothes weren't cool, and that made you feel stupid in front of your classmates." Remember not to add any of your own interpretation or judgment, but rather simply summarize what you heard them say. They may say "yes" and then keep saying more, or they may say "well, it was actually..." Keep in mind that they might not be correcting you because you got it wrong, but rather they can

see it differently now that they heard it verbalized back to them. So practice making the conversation about them, not about you. Keep leaving space for them to share without providing any solutions or correcting them. This is not about whether they are right or not. It's about you giving them the floor and being more of a listener than a contributor to the conversation. When they are finished speaking, ask them if there is anything else they would like to say about it. You could ask them how they feel or what they think. You could even ask if there is anything you can do but resist the urge to give advice or offer an assessment without them asking first. See Chapter 13 to learn about more aspects of active listening.

Conflict Resolution

Being able to resolve conflicts is a great skill, both professionally and personally. A good mediator is someone everyone approaches in times of trouble. In order to be a good mediator you need clarity of thought and a non-judgmental mindset free of biases. Listen to both sides of the story and work out a solution that works for all parties involved. Managers need to be exceptionally good at this. Those who choose jobs which call for troubleshooting on a regular basis will usually choose this kind of career because it suits their mentality and also because it is the kind of job that is best for someone who displays emotional intelligence.

They are able to put aside their own opinions and emotions and are able to resolve problems by doing this. Often people let emotions get in the way of problem solving and you may know people who do this. They give too much emotional energy to their answers and when they are proven to be wrong, get even more emotional. That helps no one.

Strategy for development: Next time you are called into a conflict situation, or you witness one in your place of work or home, take a perspective of looking for the common ground. Often when people argue about something, if you dig down deep enough, you can find common ground where they share the same values. If you can get to this, then you can help the people involved start to see how they have more in common than not. So for example, if two colleagues are in a dispute about how a project should go, encourage active listening to start. So have one person take the floor and discuss their ideas and their concerns. Then have the other person feedback to them what they heard in terms of those key ideas and concerns (without defending, modifying or denouncing). Check in with the first person that what was said was accurate. Then do this with the second person and have the first person listen and say back what they heard. Then you as the mediator can listen for where there are points of unity. So if they both talk about client satisfaction even if they have different ideas about how to get there, acknowledge "I hear you both really care that the clients are happy and that they will want to come back". When people start hearing these points of unity, they begin to see how fundamentally they are working toward the same goal. Suddenly their positions or strategies are second to this. Then see if you can brainstorm several different strategies including the ones already raised (start with those) and then see what else can be added. As you all start to work together, you build alignment and become more open to everyone hearing the other people's ideas. This type of process may take some massaging, but any steps closer to seeing how the situation is not really about one against the other is a step in the right direction toward finding a solution that works for everyone.

Tolerance

Understand that the people you interact with daily come from different walks of life and all have different backgrounds. They all have their own stories and understanding these stories helps you interact with them better. Accept their differences and value their opinions. The person who puts him or herself above others isn't being very emotionally intelligent. There are all kinds of people from whom you can learn. When you actually do sit down and learn, even who you might have once considered to be lowly have extremely valuable lessons for you. Emotionally intelligent people can read others well and will tolerate more from people of lesser intelligence because they know that even these people have a right to have an opinion. People who are less intelligent should also be easier to talk into something, and those with high emotional intelligence are able to step down to their level and see things more clearly from their point of view. It's hard to teach anything if you are biased and hold prejudices. Emotionally intelligent people don't have these biases.

Strategy for development: Ask three questions. This is a simple exercise. Next time you are with someone you don't feel you are completely on the same page as, make a point to engage with them for at least three questions. Use your active listening skills just to take in how they see things without having to convince them of anything. So if there is someone in the lunchroom that you normally wouldn't speak to, start by asking them about a new change in the company or a recent event. As they speak, find something that you can follow up with. So if they liked something or didn't like something, ask them how they would have done it differently or what would have made it better. In total,

ask three questions which gives them the experience of being an interesting person and it gives you some insight into how they see things while withholding any judgment that might crop up as they speak.

Interest

Showing interest when talking to people is essential, even more so when you're talking to someone new. When you're just starting to know someone, showing genuine interest is of great importance, or else the other person will be put off and won't feel like sharing things with you. People are good at telling when you're faking it, so be genuine and sincere. Try to ask thoughtful questions and appreciate the answers. Also remember dates and names, as it shows people you actually care.

Strategy for development: Start with physical cues that you are interested in the person. This means you stand or sit with your shoulders and toes pointing toward them. This is a nonverbal cue that lets people know you are interested and are paying attention. Then apply your active listening skills.

Flexibility

You can't behave with everyone in the same way in every situation. Different times call for different behavior, and you need to be flexible in that regard. Some situations may require you to be really soft, like talking to your daughter about her heartbreak. Another situation may need you to be really stern. You have to understand that different situations require different attitudes, and sometimes, you have to bend your own rules in order to maintain successful relationships.

Take every situation as it happens and if it leaves you with a negative experience, you need to work out why. Emotionally developed people are able to look objectively at problems and understand where the lack of communication came into the picture. They don't hurl blame at others. They simply acknowledge that there is a problem and try to solve it.

Strategy for development: Think of something that is currently unresolved between yourself and another person. This could be a small tiff you had with your spouse or when you walked out of a meeting without completing a conversation for example. Go back to the other person involved and let them know that something seems incomplete and that you would like to hear them out and/or resolve it. Acknowledge if you were not good with them or if you were impatient. People love to hear this and often respect you more for following up with a problem head on. Ask them what else they wanted to say about the topic. Then if there is anything to do with the issue at hand, ask how they suggest you can move forward. Consider their strategy and let them know what they should expect of you. Sometimes it is as simple as letting them know that next time you will respond to their email within a couple of days (in case they were feeling ignored) or that you will listen to their ideas fully before changing the subject. Other times, it might mean you commit to a certain action like taking your husband out on a date or being on time for a meeting. Once you make these commitments, honor your word and have integrity. This means you make sure to follow through. If you don't, go back to the person to clean it up and make a new commitment. Hiding from your mistakes or your missteps only tells other people that you are not a strong leader or a person of integrity. Admitting when things aren't working and taking action and responsibility to transform them is a sign of great leadership and ultimately, workability in your interpersonal relationships.

Good Judgement

Listening to your gut is important, and heeding it can improve your judgement. You should pay attention to what your instinct says. Some of us are not good at this, and while your gut may not always be right, it's important that you don't silence it. Instead, what you should do is hone your observation and judgement skills. Look around and learn from your environment. Pay attention to what people say, what they do, how they act in different circumstances, and then analyze what works best. Attention to detail is the best thing you can have.

You have something called intuition for a good reason. Although emotionally intelligent people know that the hunches that they get generally mean something, they don't jump to conclusions. They merely use their intuition as a guide to logical conclusions backed up by whatever is needed to improve the situation. They adapt and don't let their emotions get in the way of progress.

Strategy for development: The next time you have a hunch about the next steps or the right thing to do in a situation, test it verbally with the others involved. Don't be forceful, only exploratory. For example, if something is going awry with planning for an upcoming event, you might say "I have a hunch that we might want to take a different approach that helps address our issue with [X Y Z]. Could it be useful to try [X]?" This is a gentle way to test your intuition and have other people consider the idea without putting them on the defensive or negating any other ideas that have already been offered.

Persuasiveness

To be able to conduct good or successful business, you have to be good at the art of persuasion. It's not something only sales people need, it's a skill everyone can benefit from. It's not always about selling something material; you may even need to sell someone on your idea, or a service. Promotion requires persuasion, and so does pitching your project. You need to be convincing, strong, and confident.

The same amount of persuasiveness can be even used in relationships, making it a wonderful skill to have. Never walk over the ideas of others, but try to incorporate them into your solutions. That way, everybody comes out of the situation feeling whole.

Strategy for development: Look for what the other person can benefit from in the scenario. Ask them questions about what matters to them and listen for what problems they are facing that your idea or product can help solve. It will occur to them in a different way than with selling. It's about you looking for the match between their problem and your solution.

Open-mindedness

It's great to have supreme confidence in your ideas and opinions, but at the same time, you have to be careful not to disrespect someone else's opinions. It's important that you keep an open mind and listen to what your peers have to say. Following their advice and suggestions is up to you, but respecting them is not debatable. The people you interact with need to feel that their suggestions and feedback are valued. The best CEOs are those who have learned the value of listening. Emotionally intelligent people are able to use listening and open-mindedness together in order to actually achieve what their initial aims are. They are not afraid to change an idea if someone finds fault with it. In fact, they are more likely to give praise when it is due and develop even closer bonds with their coworkers or their friends because of this honest way of thinking.

Strategy for development: Take an idea to a meeting with the goal to let the group take ownership of it. This means that you don't enter a meeting with an attachment to the concept that you have the best idea. This means you enter a meeting giving the idea to the group. You are part of the group, and you get to help shape the idea, but if the idea takes a whole new turn, be active in supporting the new path. Ask for feedback and input that helps inject new life into the idea. By the time the meeting is over, the idea may look completely differently than what you started with. Take time to acknowledge everyone who contributed to it and thank them for making it better. Moving from a space of attachment to a space of commitment is freeing for yourself and the others involved. It means you are committed to a certain solution or outcome, but you are open to finding a path that works for everyone in getting there. You engage, but you don't dominate.

Sense of Humor

A great sense of humor can take you far in life. You must have realized at some point that people are drawn to funny personalities. Humorous people generate a certain aura that attracts others. Humor can work like magic to lighten up serious situations and diffuse the tension. People love to laugh. So if you can, try to cultivate a good sense of humor that you can use to your advantage. You'll have to do a lot of trial and error, but it's well worth the effort. However, it's important to remember to not be insensitive or offensive when using humor.

Humor helps you to get through many of the battles in life. Working in a hospice at one time, an individual I consider to be a friend used her sense of fun to actually make the environment for the workers and patients not only tolerable but also positive. That's real emotional intelligence at work!

Strategy for development: Enter your next social situation with a smile on your face. Lead with something light such as a funny personal anecdote from earlier in the day. When someone speaks, follow up with a joke that elevates them. So if someone speaks about their child who has a messy room, you might joke "thank goodness they can't turn back time to see how we were as kids, right?!" You might get a chuckle. Even if they follow up by saying they were actually really clean as kids, you can simply laugh. The whole mood will be bright, and others will be encouraged to be light-hearted as well.

Good Manners

The importance of good manners is much underplayed. People don't talk about this much, but "Manners maketh a man." Simple things like saying "please" and "thank you" can take your relationships far. People will be pleased to talk to you. Always behave with polished manners, just remember not to smother people.

Strategy for development: Practice following up "thank you" with "for..." This is simple but can make other people feel acknowledged for their work or effort in a much more impactful way. So if you are in a restaurant setting, you could say to the waiter "thank you for a delicious meal today. I'm so satisfied." Or after a meeting, you could say to a colleague, "thank you for your thoughts on this. I'm really pleased to get your perspective before I move to the next phase". Sometimes these moments of adding a little more to a simple thank you can make people feel more affinity toward you. When people feel good about themselves because of your small gestures or compliments, they will associate that good feeling with you.

Supportiveness

Supporting people you know is very important because it shows them you care. People really like it when the people they feel close to or look up to support them in their endeavors. It boosts their confidence when someone else believes in them, too. So always be motivating and supportive of the people around you and stay enthusiastic. People will want to stick around with you more.

Strategy for development: Right now think of three people in your life who are up to something, taking on a project or trying something new. This could be a diet, a new sport, reading a new book, changing positions at work, doing a volunteer project or something of the like. Even by text, a note or a short phone call, reach out to follow up with them and take an interest. Tell them that you've been thinking about them and wondering how it's going. If you are proud of them or impressed by what they are doing, share that. If you feel inspired to offer help or participate with them, this can be a great way to really let them know you support them. However, sometimes a simple note or text can suffice to have them feel supported by you. It doesn't have to take much time, but it can make a big difference for them feeling that they have people who care about them.

Chapter 12:

Easy Ways to Improve Interpersonal Skills at Work

A happy face fixes (almost) everything

What's common between all the people who are the life of the party? They are happy. If you maintain an upbeat attitude and smile often, your coworkers will like you more and will be drawn toward you. This is basic psychology. Also remember that whenever you're having a bad day, don't take it out on others and don't try to pull them down with you. Your negative emotions are not something worth sharing. Your positive ones are because they lift people up and make them happier.

Show that you care

Always show your coworkers that you care. If someone performs well, make sure you praise him or her and don't hold back the applause. Appreciate coworkers when they do something right, even if it's something small, and thank them for it. Take the time to know your colleagues and identify at least one quality you admire in them. When you let them know about it, they will feel much more warmth for you. Showing others that you care motivates them to do the same and put in their best work.

Be considerate

Spend some time with your colleagues and take note of what's going on in their personal lives. Congratulate them on their achievements and happy events, be it a kid's graduation or a birthday party. Show compassion when they are in a bad situation or have suffered a tragedy. Use first names to refer to people and look them in the eye when talking to them. Show them you value their opinions and their input.

Be an active listener

You must have heard of this plenty of times, but let me reiterate it: Don't listen to respond, listen to understand. That is what being an active listener means, and sadly, it is becoming a lost art. An active listener shows the speaker he or she intends to both hear and recognize the other person's opinions. Really think about what the other person says and *then* respond so he or she knows you have actually taken the time to form a genuine response. People feel more connected to active listeners.

Promote togetherness

Create a friendly and helpful environment to let your colleagues thrive in the workplace. Don't create a personal hierarchy by treating people differently. Treat everyone the same, irrespective of what their position is, and value their opinions the same. Always promote a feeling of togetherness and discourage gossip. When you address a crowd, take time to ensure that you've been understood properly. This will tell others you're a team player and can be trusted.

Settle disputes

Be the person who brings people together. Whenever a dispute arises in your workplace; people will know whom to approach to resolve it. Don't let a dispute between two colleagues be the reason for the whole team's bad mood. Take the mantle of a moderator and improve the situation in every way you can. Discuss things with both parties and arrange for them to talk in a neutral setting with you moderating the exchange. This will help resolve the conflict and your office will be a happier place. It will also reinforce your position as a leader.

Hone your communication skills

You don't just need to be an active listener; you also have to possess good communication skills that help you convey your thoughts both easily and elaborately. When you are discussing things with other people at work, take time to think about what you want to say and what words you want to use. Don't just blurt what comes to your mind first. When your communication is clearer, you'll avoid misunderstandings. You will be perceived as mature and intelligent if you speak well. Don't give voice to half-baked thoughts.

Make them laugh

There's a reason why funny people are so popular and well liked. If you have a good sense of humor, use it to your advantage. This can be tricky, but as long as you don't make any inappropriate jokes or laugh off any serious issues, you'll be just fine. Using humor effectively is a great way to defuse some tension and even break down barriers shy

or moody people present.

Put yourself in their shoes

You have to be able to understand how someone else is feeling in his or her situation. Sometimes, a coworker may not be performing well or may be failing at something. Instead of giving them a hard time about it, it's better to think about what they might be going through and then talk to them. You may think of one thing as the correct solution, but for someone else, that might not be the right solution. You have to display empathy and keep check of your own feelings.

Stop whining

There are people who complain chronically and do little to solve things, and then there are people who work to make things better. Don't be the former, because they are not very well liked in the office, or anywhere else really. You are essentially emanating negativity in the office when you complain about things unnecessarily, and this pushes others away from you. When something is troubling you too much, write about it somewhere, or have a brief exchange about it with someone in your friends or family. Don't constantly complain in the office, or you'll become the office brat.

Chapter 13:
Active Listening

Listening is a basic fundamental of effective communication, so you need to hone your listening skills in order to get better at communicating. We have talked about how active listening can help you. Now let's take a look at what active listening really is all about.

Active listening means really *listening* attentively to the other person instead of just hearing it passively. There's a big difference. Active listening makes use of all five senses while listening, and you have to actually look like you're listening interestedly to the other person.

There are some generic signs that inform the other person you are listening actively. They can change slightly depending on the culture or the circumstance but you need to keep them in mind.

Smile

Smiling from time to time can help affirm you are paying attention to the other person. You can smile while agreeing with them and nodding while doing so reinforces it.

Eye Contact

Keeping a good amount of eye contact with the speaker is encouraging. Sometimes it can be intimidating, but with smiles and other nonverbal messages, you can avoid that.

Posture

Maintaining attentive posture is important. A good listener leans forward slightly and tilts his head to the side at times to show his interest.

Mirroring

Sometimes, mirroring the other person's posture and facial expressions can also help affirm you are listening attentively by showing empathy.

Positive Reinforcement

If you use phrases like "good", "yes", or "indeed" sparingly while listening to someone, it encourages them. It is better to follow it by saying why you agree with them.

Questioning

Questioning the other person can also help sometimes. Make sure you ask thoughtful questions and not unnecessarily irritating ones. Also make sure you ask at a moment that is not distracting to the speaker.

Summarization

When the speaker is done speaking, you can repeat what they told you in a short summary. This shows that you were actually listening to them and gives them an opportunity to correct you if you missed anything.

Ways to Deal with Difficult People

Now that we have talked about the skills you need to possess in order to improve your emotional intelligence, let's talk about some ways you can deal with especially difficult people. This way you can cut out any unnecessary negativity or stress from your life.

1. Establish boundaries

First of all, realize that you cannot please everyone and you cannot meet everyone's expectations. If you spend your life trying to live up to people's expectations, you will always feel inadequate. An emotionally intelligent person always sets some boundaries and maintains a degree of emotional distance from difficult people.

2. Focus on solutions

Instead of focusing on a problem a difficult person poses, an emotionally intelligent person chooses to focus his energy on finding a solution. Arguing with a troublemaker is fruitless and you will only invite negativity. You should instead try to look for a solution to the problem.

3. **Know your positive and negative aspects**

Emotionally intelligent people are very self-aware. They know where they can excel and where they won't. The knowledge of their strengths and flaws helps them find the right path for themselves. It also helps them manage the stress from an unreasonable person.

4. **Don't forget**

Experience is regarded as the best teacher and an emotionally intelligent person is well aware of this. Such a person doesn't forget about the type of troubles a difficult person poses and avoids all future exchanges to avoid another difficult situation. They learn from their experiences.

5. **Terminate negative talk**

Difficult and unreasonable people are always saying negative things. They will criticize for no reason and find a flaw in almost anything. You don't need that kind of negativity in your life; don't listen to them unless you absolutely must. Instead, try to engage yourself in meaningful and positive conversations.

6. **Don't consume yourself in a fight**

As an emotionally intelligent person, you must realize an argument or quarrel with a difficult person will leave you exhausted and with little results to show. Instead, conserve your energy and strength for another day and a more fruitful task. Realize you don't always have to respond to a difficult person's negative comments.

7. Focus on your joys

Be happy with what you have and stay happy because you get to do the things you love. Derive your satisfaction from within rather than relying on an external source to give it to you. An emotionally intelligent person doesn't let other people's opinions of him influence him.

8. You deserve a rest

Rest is important for you, not only to recharge your physical self but also your mental self. An emotionally intelligent person realizes this and gets the rest he deserves. This reduces stress and keeps him positive and creative to take on the next day.

9. Cling to like-minded people for support

Dealing with difficult people takes a mental toll, so it's important that you forge the right support system for yourself and stay with a group of like-minded people to recharge your mental batteries. These people support you through tough situations and help you stay positive.

10. Stay above problematic situations

You don't have to get involved in emotional brawls with

difficult people. Instead, you should put forward your arguments with facts and numbers. Don't focus on things you cannot control; find solutions that include factors you *can* control.

11. **Forgive**

As an emotionally intelligent person, you should realize the importance of forgiving others and yourself. Learn from the mistakes of the past and adapt yourself to circumstances. It doesn't mean forgetting, but rather letting go of things so you can move on. Look forward to accomplishing new things instead of focusing on past failures.

12. **Disconnect**

Sometimes you will have to refrain from reacting and just disconnect from everything. If you want to get out of yourself, you will need to disengage, take time to recharge, and get rid of all the negative energy.

13. **Limit your caffeine intake**

Caffeine is something you should definitely cut down if you want to stay in control of your emotions. It triggers the release of adrenaline, which is responsible for the fight or flight response of your body. You don't want to act impulsively, so you should cut down on your caffeine intake. This will help you avoid responding to a negative comment by a difficult person and help in letting go more easily.

Chapter 14:

Applying the Wisdom of the Ages

So many great thinkers in the realm of philosophy have brought ideas to the table that can be applied to emotional intelligence. Their research, wisdom, and search for knowledge have quality relevance in the context of this conversation. A selection of philosophies is detailed below for your reflection. Each philosopher or school of philosophy can provide new insights that bring the concept of emotional intelligence to life.

Stoicism

Stoicism is a school of Greek philosophy best known for the emphasis on emotions leading to errors in personal judgment. This clearly maps onto emotional intelligence in the sense that when someone gives weight to their destructive emotions without being conscious and considered, they can precipitate errors in their judgment that may lead to poor actions. If you think of the common understanding of the word stoic, you may picture a peaceful, calm, contemplative person. Stoicism would advocate for this type of calm presence that is not reactionary. To live well from a stoic's perspective is to be aware of one's emotions, be reflective on these emotions and still act in a way that is appropriate. Stoics would promote living with a sense of self-control while using logic to make decisions and take actions rather than relying on emotions.

Epicureanism

Epicureanism is another system of ancient Greek philosophy that emphasized the pursuit of pleasure as the most important goal in life. In this school of philosophy, the absence of fear and pain were the key components of pleasure. A simple life was considered good, and pleasure was mostly a sensation of the mind rather than a physical sensation. Our emotional experience of life resides in the mind. Epicureanism can be linked to our modern conceptions of emotional intelligence through this sense of being present to states of the mind and being conscious of one's emotional and mental experiences of life. We cannot pursue a good life and a pleasurable mental existence if we are not emotionally intelligent and aware of our emotions.

Descartes

Descartes theorized that a part of the brain (the pineal gland) would send signals throughout the nervous system which then incited the body to react in different ways. So for him, the root of emotion was based in the brain, and the body reacted based on natural processes. Many philosophers and psychologists since have fallen in line with the perspective that the brain (not necessarily this part of the brain) is the root of our emotions and the impetus for us to behave in certain ways. In this context, emotional intelligence is the process of stopping that automatic process of the brain-body-action sequence and engaging in a more conscious way. We can witness the urges that we are drawn to that are based on the emotions we are feeling, and then we can choose to mindfully follow that urge or instead choose a different path.

Aristotle

Aristotle wrote about emotions in the context of using them to a moral end. He wrote that people can work on developing themselves to know when to use the correct emotions in the correct circumstances. When translating this into a lesson in becoming an expert in emotional intelligence, we can consider what is emotionally appropriate. Again, this begins with awareness of our emotions and being literate of other's emotional experiences at the moment as well. As we observe our emotional state, we can see the cues that link back to our morals or core values. We can then read a situation based on how the circumstance complies with or is an affront to our core values. Our emotions can often be a quick mechanism to test if these values are being supported (in the case of joy, happiness, affinity) or challenged (in the case of fear, anger, frustration). With a high level of emotional intelligence, we can use these emotional cues to explore our inner state of mind and then appropriately articulate real issues in a manner that is respectful and effective.

Plato

In The Republic, Plato's most famous work, he speaks about one component of the mind being the emotive part. He also acknowledges two other components of the mind, which he defines as the reasoning and the desiring parts. This can shed light on the idea that even though our emotions can call us into quick action at times, there are other tools or aspects of our brains that can also be helpful in decision-making. By being emotionally intelligent and cognizant of our changing emotions, we can also compare them against these other aspects of our brains. Especially in consideration of reason and logic, we can slow our emotionally based reactions in order to balance these against each other. Looking at where the emotions and logic meet can help guide us to be appropriate with our decisions that affect others and ourselves.

Hume

Hume spoke about how emotions, among other aspects of a person, were central to the character. He validated the notion that emotions have great utility and are a critical aspect of an individual. Through becoming emotionally intelligent, we raise to the level of awareness of our core personality. We learn to acknowledge our emotional experience as part of our core selves. We can look for the utility of our emotions in defining our life decisions moving forward and being true to ourselves.

Spinoza

Baruch Spinoza, a Dutch philosopher, spoke of emotions in terms of how they can help draw someone toward a certain action or away. So he was emphasizing the utility of emotional experiences to influence behavior. In the context of emotional intelligence, this is a useful perspective. Our emotions are not to be smothered or denied. Rather, as we are more emotionally intelligent, we are able to recognize our emotions as they emerge. We are able to gain clues about what is happening in that current moment based on our emotional response. We can use these clues to help us act and react. Often emotions emerge from thoughts that are sometimes unconscious. Our brains are always processing our surroundings. When we have an emotional reaction to something, it is often a function of our brains doing high-level processing without us being consciously aware of it. When we are aware of our emotions, we can trace back to our mental processes and reflect on what thoughts would have lead us to those emotional occurrences. This is very high-level functioning and can lead us to be successful in our interactions with others as well. By being able to name our emotions and also explain why we are experiencing those emotions and/or why we feel called to act in certain ways, we display a high level of cognitive functioning as well as self-awareness.

Solomon

Robert Solomon was a contemporary American professor and researcher of philosophy. He theorized that not only are humans not stuck with emotions as they arise, but cognitive processes can be applied to the experience of emotions that can insert reason as well as fundamentally shift those emotions. This malleability of emotions points to the concept of personal control. So emotions may arise naturally in the body, but we do not need to accept them as is or act only in reaction to these natural experiences. We can apply conscious thinking, look for why we have these emotions, decide if we want to act with these emotions as the source and also choose to modify the experience if we want. Those who are emotionally intelligent can learn from their emotional experience yet take charge of how they will react. They have self-regulation that allows them to be aware of their experience yet be fully mindful in determining how to outwardly act or even how to conceive mentally of their experience.

Chapter 15:

Worksheets and Exercises

Developing emotional intelligence is a process. It takes practice and awareness. Be generous with yourself along the journey. Many of us have acted directly from our emotions for much of our lives, without bringing to conscious awareness the catalyst for why those emotions arose. As we become more mindful of what is happening to our bodies and minds, we are still bound to fall into old habits of acting without thinking. When we can reflect on these behaviors, we can learn and grow. Nothing is 100% and sometimes our emotions come on so strong that we find ourselves acting and even surprising ourselves. This is a practice. It doesn't happen overnight. The below exercises are intended to give you tools in order to develop into an emotionally intelligent person. As you grow, you become more effective in your own self-regulation, and you also become more effective socially. Putting in a little time day by day can spell great results in terms of your own life satisfaction as well as the results you can achieve with others.

Exercise: Tracking - Your Emotional Log (1 day)

Before looking to modify your behavior or improve your interactions with others, the first step is to simply observe yourself. Observe what emotions arise over the course of a typical day and observe how you act in response to these emotions. Below, simply record the various activities and situations you find yourself in, as well as the emotions you experience, followed by your actions or reactions in that situation. This exercise of bringing to awareness and naming your reactions can help you see your patterns, triggers and the connection between your own emotions and the way you act.

At the end of the day review this sheet and look for insights. Did you get upset in crowded situations? Did you feel joy when you were around your kids? Did you act compassionately toward yourself and others consistently? This is not about evaluating your emotions or behavior. This is simply about taking a moment to reflect on the link between your emotions, circumstances, and behaviors. If you see an opportunity to do something differently in the future, you could make yourself a note, make a plan or journal about it, but the main objective of this exercise is developing awareness.

Instructions:

For one day, list your activities from morning until night, the context or situation, the emotions you experienced (name them), the physical experience of the emotions and your reaction or response to the situation.

Activity | Context/Situation | Emotions | Physical experience | Reaction/Response Example:
Took bus to work, crowded situation and warm, frustrated, fidgeting/heart racing, retreated, kept eyes down and didn't engage with others

Notes — list here what insights arise as you review your daily log:

Exercise 2: Mapping Triggers

To become an expert in emotional intelligence, you must continually raise your awareness of your own emotional state. There are many theories on how emotions arise in humans, but it is most useful to understand your own personal process. Triggers are things that happen in your environment that might incite you to have a certain emotion — positive, negative or otherwise. By becoming more aware of our triggers, we can be more prepared for these emotions to arise and we can become better self-regulators.

Instructions:

This exercise involves taking 15–30 minutes to reflect on some of the core human emotions and what triggers in your environment elicit those emotions in you. Triggers can be physical situations, certain people, certain climates, and so forth. Think about all of your five senses to help you discover your various triggers.

Happiness:

Sadness:

Fear:

Anger:

Surprise:

Disgust:

Choose one trigger from the above list that leads you to act in a way that you are not pleased about. List the trigger here: Explain how you behave in response to that trigger:

Consider 3 different responses you could take next time you are faced with that trigger:

1)

2)

3)

Choose one trigger from the above list that leads to a positive, desirable experience in your life. List the trigger here:

Explain how you behave in response to that trigger:

What makes the experience desirable?

What is your strategy to elicit that experience in the near future? (i.e. should you call someone to set up a visit, book a family vacation or buy a new book?)

Exercise 3: Body Sensations

In line with becoming more aware of our mind-body connection, our body can provide us many clues as to our emotional and mental states. Many of us spend our days in highly intellectual spaces. We want to look smart. We are constantly thinking and strategizing. We often are only conscious of our bodies if something is off. We might notice pain, discomfort or stiffness. Our bodies can be a great source of information and insight. As we take the time to mindfully consider the cues our bodies can provide us, we become more expert in emotional intelligence. We get to know ourselves and through being excellent self-observers, we become highly capable of acting appropriately regardless of what our emotions alert us to. We also can use our knowledge of our emotions to trace back to what is working or not working for us more accurately in any situation that elicits an emotional response. From this awareness, we can learn to be tactful and articulate in a way that can be understood, accepted and even welcomed by others.

Instructions:

Start by writing the top 5-10 emotions that color your life (the main ones you experience):

1)

2)

3)

4)

5)

6)

7)

8)

9)

10)

Use the space below to draw a rough outline of your body. Consider each of the above emotions, one at a time. Where do these emotions get expressed in your physical self and how? You can draw arrows, use words or colors to capture your physical experience of each one of these emotions. Drawing conscious awareness of these named emotions and where they emerge in the body allows you to identify your reactions faster and more clearly. From there you can mindfully decide how to respond as opposed to reacting without awareness.

Exercise 4: Body to Mind Power

In the above exercise, we looked at how our bodily cues can help us become cognitively aware of what is happening in our emotional state. This exercise tackles the flip side of that connection. Here we are looking at how using our bodies in different ways can, in fact, elicit a certain emotional and cognitive state of being. Lots of research has shown that when we put our bodies in certain positions and certain states, we can influence our emotions and cognitive path. This is taking what we are learning about body language and using it on ourselves and to our own advantage. We are likely becoming pretty attuned to other people's body language at this point, so turn that observation around on yourself.

Instructions:

Start by thinking about a peak experience for you. What are your emotions in that experience?

Describe your body (your posture, your shape, etc.):

The next time you are feeling a loss of power, confidence, love, or another desired emotion, try re-creating that physical experience and observe how your emotional state may begin to shift. In some ways, this seems a little phony at first. However, our bodies and minds are entirely connected. The feedback loop goes both ways. When our emotional state is low, we often find our bodies in predictable positions (head low, shoulders curled forward, slouching and so forth). When we put our bodies in ways that match highly emotional experiences, our emotional state and mind will be cued to a new direction. We will head down new neural pathways that have us ruminate in memories and other experiences where we were in that same physical state. Suddenly we experience our thinking shifting more to the positive and powerful, and our emotions follow suit.

Next, write down emotional states that you would like to have more control over (those that you wish you experienced less or that had less of an impact on your quality of life). Below write the emotion, then a counter emotion. A counter emotion is something that feels opposite to the first emotion. So if the second emotion is present, the first one is rarely present at the same time (like joy and despair). The third part is to put your body in a pose, position or physical state that is consistent with this counter emotion. Hold it for 30 seconds to one minute.

Undesirable emotion:

Counter emotion:

Physical expression of the counter emotion: Undesirable emotion:

Counter emotion:

Physical expression of the counter emotion:

Undesirable emotion:

Counter emotion:

Physical expression of the counter emotion:

Undesirable emotion:

Counter emotion:

Physical expression of the counter emotion:

Undesirable emotion:

Counter emotion:

Physical expression of the counter emotion:

Exercise 5: Cleaning Up and Being Conscious

A sign of great leadership and high emotional intelligence is to take responsibility for any times when we acted or reacted in ways that were not ideal. Not only does taking responsibility clear the air with the others involved but it also elevates you as a person of integrity. Further, it creates an atmosphere where people don't have to be perfect, but they can take action to make things better after the fact. This is one of the more challenging exercises, but it's also one of the exercises that can amplify your leadership and emotional intelligence most rapidly and effectively.

Instructions:

Consider recent events (even going back 5 years if things are still lingering, unfinished or in bad shape) and think about times when you reacted to something from an emotional space without being conscious or deliberate.

Consider who was involved and what their experience was like. This means taking an empathetic view of the situation and considering how the experience was for them, what emotions it may have elicited for them and how they may be now. Think of any other results or even missed opportunities that have resulted because of your behavior.

Situation 1:

How I reacted:

Who was involved:

How I left them feeling:

State of things now (How has your relationship changed? What other outcomes came directly or indirectly because of my behavior?):

Situation 2:

How I reacted:

Who was involved? How I left them feeling:
State of things now (How has your relationship changed?
What other outcomes came directly or indirectly because of
my behavior?):

Situation 3: How I reacted:
Who was involved?

How I left them feeling:

State of things now (How has your relationship changed?
What other outcomes came directly or indirectly because of
my behavior?):

Now consider how you will clean up that experience. This
involved four steps: 1) Taking responsibility for your actions
without blaming or excusing; 2) Acknowledging how you may
have made the other person feel and what their experience
may have been like; 3) Listening to them for their experience
and their reflections (active listening and not defending); and
4) Asking them and listening for new solutions, then agreeing
on what is acceptable or what can be committed to for the
future. Some may modify this by adding in a "sorry" or even
letting the other person know you are working on becoming a
more emotionally intelligent person. Even though there are
lots of reasons to justify your behavior or reaction, that does

not help you become a better leader. Taking responsibility is always the foundation for workability and integrity. It always continuously reinforces to you and others that you have a say in your behavior. You get to choose it. You get to be responsible for it. You are in charge. It's your turn now to consider how each of the three situations above can be addressed. Remember that the other person can react or respond in any way. You are not doing this to feel good or to look good. You are doing this as part of your process to develop a stronger emotional intelligence and in becoming an expert leader. It's not always easy or fun. However, you may be very pleased with some of the new relationships that emerge and doors that open as a result of this work.

Situation 1 – I will take the following action(s) to address my behavior (list people, approach, script your key messages and identify a timeline to do this):

Situation 2 – I will take the following action(s) to address my behavior (list people, approach, script your key messages and identify a timeline to do this):

Situation 2 – I will take the following action(s) to address my behavior (list people, approach, script your key messages and identify a timeline to do this):

Now do it!

Exercise 6: Focusing on Others

A high emotional intelligence means not only being excellent at your own emotional awareness and self-regulation but also perceptive to others. Experts with high emotional intelligence are able to identify emotions in others, triggers and even influence others' emotional states.

Instructions:

Consider the 10 key people in your life. Choose a selection of people from your family, your friend groups, your professional life, your community and others. Think of the people you spend the most time with, those that are closest to you, those that contribute to your life and those that have a lot of influence and impact on your quality of life. List them below and identify one action (even small) that you can take to positively influence their emotional state of being. This could range from a compliment to a gift or an offer to help with something that matters to them. People who are highly emotionally intelligent dig in and take an interest in others. They hone their skills at noticing other people's reactions too. Take a moment to do something that is genuine (research shows that a compliment that is far-fetched can actually leave people feeling worse about themselves) and that has significance to each person individually. This is a way for you to develop stronger empathy and to focus on others. Research in the realm of positive psychology emphasizes that a key element of life satisfaction is putting energy and focus into others. So by doing this exercise, you are really helping everyone involved, including yourself.

Person:

Action I can take to enhance their emotional experience:

Person:

Action I can take to enhance their emotional experience:
Person:

Action I can take to enhance their emotional experience:

Person:

Action I can take to enhance their emotional experience:

Person:

Action I can take to enhance their emotional experience:

Person:

Action I can take to enhance their emotional experience:

Person:

Action I can take to enhance their emotional experience:

Person:

Action I can take to enhance their emotional experience:

Person:

Action I can take to enhance their emotional experience:

Person:

Action I can take to enhance their emotional experience:

Conclusion

With that, we have reached the end of this book. I sincerely hope you found this book useful and I wish you all the very best in all endeavors of your life. Always keep a positive approach and don't forget to practice the exercises outlined in this book. You will be a better person for it. With your continued practice you will find your emotional intelligence growing as a direct result of being aware of its existence as you use it to the make your life and your relationships with others better.

You'll get there. Thanks for reading.

CPSIA information can be obtained
at www.ICGtesting.com
Printed in the USA
LVHW052017100221
678950LV00013B/1476

9 781914 253485